A BRIDGE INTO MISSION

A BRIDGE INTO MISSION

One person's experiences, thought and feelings while serving our
RISEN LORD JESUS

and a Complete and Comprehensive list of
"CONSTRUCTION-INSTRUCTIONS" for
Mission Trip Preparations

The story of a mission that brought "HOPE" to
people in the small forgotten Country of Moldova

By

Woody Woodward

A division of Squire Publishers, Inc.
4500 College Blvd.
Leawood, KS 66211
1/888/888-7696

A division of Squire Publishers, Inc.
4500 College Blvd.
Leawood, KS 66211
1/888/888-7696

WHAT ABOUT THE COVER?

My wife and I discussed the magnitude of the message to be portrayed on the cover. After much consideration and prayer we felt that the title of the book should be artistically conveyed to allow the reader a glimpse of what **A BRIDGE INTO MISSION** is actually about.

What does the cover of this book say to you?

This is a description of what my precious wife felt the Holy Spirit was trying to convey through her prayers. Using colored pencils, the globe was drawn allowing North America, the vast expanse of the Atlantic Ocean, and finally most of Eastern Europe to be visible. The bridge-like structure begins in the middle of the United States, right about where Kansas City, Missouri is located, arches upward across the great Atlantic and lands approximately in the center of Moscow.

We did not want to actually label these two great cities on the cover because this book is not just about a mission trip back and forth from only these two places. We also did not want the cover design to be generated on a computer. You see, God does not use a computer to design and plan HIS perfect will for our lives; HE uses HIS own nail-scarred hands to draw the detailed sketches of life that we follow or reject at our own choosing. It is this hand-sketched look that we want to convey to all who decide to investigate the message contained between the two covers of this book.

We also asked the artist to place the image of

Christ's nail-pierced outstretched hands, not actually touching the earth, but formed in such a way that they are positioned around the earth, gently cradling the world. We are trying to paint a mental picture that Christ's hands are constantly around us and HE is forever there when we need His gentle touch. HE never holds us so tightly that we are not allowed to stumble, but we will never fall beyond His tender and vigilant reach.

In his loving outstretched hands may all of us rest, and in HIS loving peace and comfort we will all rejoice.

Woody Woodward

A STATEMENT FROM THE AUTHOR

Dear Reader,

I have been in thoughtful prayer about what should be said about the main purpose for writing this book. It is my heart's desire that anyone who has ever had a desire or even an interest in building a mission team for a mission project view this book as "a must read!" I believe this book can be a very helpful tool for any church that desires to get active in mission work, but might not know where or how to begin.

My earnest prayer is that this book will be read and understood as much more than just a story about a fascinating mission trip. I hope to create in the mind of the reader a vision that allows everyone to see how the Word of God came alive for us as we traveled from village to village teaching and preaching the simple life-changing truths that are found in HIS Word. In new Moldova or in old Antioch, when one is following the direction and the leading of God's Holy Spirit, anyone can minister by the same means as those first 11 faithful but very inexperienced followers of Christs did.

I want the reader to understand that regardless of gifts or qualifications or lack thereof, **everyone can be an effective and powerful witnesss** for Christ. We don't need all the answers. All we need is a willing and caring heart that allows God to use our hands and our feet to accomplish HIS purpose. *One does not have to be a full-time foreign missionary to be an effective full-time missionary for Christ.* Fulfilling the Great Commission is every believer's responsibility, no matter where we might be called to serve.

Following the path of writing a book was one I never dreamed that I would ever have ventured onto. I only desire that the Lord direct my thoughts and my every step. I pray that you will be blessed and encouraged in your walk with the Lord Jesus as you read and begin to build your own **BRIDGE INTO MISSION**. Proverbs 16:3, "Commit yourself to the Lord and your plans will be established."

Woody Woodward

PREFACE

Dear Reader,

I am neither a pastor nor a great evangelist. I never graduated from college. I am merely a lay person who loves Christ and strives to serve HIM daily. My passion is for seeing people everywhere come to know the LORD, not only as their Savior but also as their best and truest, most understanding and faithful friend.

The purpose of this book is simple. I want to impress upon each and every one of you this profound fact: **"One does not have to be a full-time foreign missionary to be an effective full-time missionary for Christ."** What I hope you discover as you read of our experiences on this remarkable mission trip is that every believer can be and must be a missionary for Christ. Where has the Lord established your mission field? Mine happens to be in the former Soviet Union. I hope this book can help you find yours.

My intent was to "live the Scriptures" as we traveled from village to village taking HIS "Good News" to people who had never even heard the precious name of Jesus. I was the first American that many of these spiritually hungry souls had ever met. Many of the historical facts used in this book were not gleaned from textbooks. Many have never been told before. Numerous stories of the terrible persecution for being a Christian in Russia before the fall of Communism have never been written about. I will share facts as honestly and accurately as they were conveyed to me and as witnessed first hand. I ask for forgiveness should my efforts appear to fail in that regard.

I am grateful for a wonderful Christ-centered church and a truly amazing pastor, Reverend Adam Hamilton. The members of the United Methodist Church of the Resurrection of Leawood, Kansas, and our pastor have a true heart and a passionate vision for mission work both at home and abroad. I express my deepest appreciation to all who encouraged me to turn my daily journal writings into a book. I pray that with the leadership of God's Holy Spirit, this book will help you begin to discover what you need to begin building your own **BRIDGE INTO MISSION**.

I express my humble gratitude to my dear friends and brothers in the Lord, Pavel Horev and Wilhelm Dick. These two wonderful Christians have helped my wife, Cheri, and me experience a unique and growing ministry with the beautiful Russian-speaking people. With the HOLY SPIRIT's never-ending help, Cheri and I both changed our ideas and thinking about words like tolerance, acceptance and unconditional love.

My greatest "thank you" goes to my beloved and supportive wife, Cheri. Without her patience and constant dedication to reading, rereading and making grammatical corrections, this book would have never been more than just a dream and an unfulfilled vision.

Please join me as we begin this walk together through the daily construction phases of a life-changing **BRIDGE INTO MISSION**!

Woody Woodward

DAY 1

Dearest Brothers and Sisters in Christ at the
United Methodist Church of the Resurrection (COR),
and around the globe,

I begin each day with a Scripture verse.

*"And for this reason I remind you to kindle afresh the
gift of God which is in you through the laying on of my hands.
For God has not given us a spirit of fear, but of power and
love and sound mind. Therefore do not be ashamed of the
testimony of our Lord, or of me HIS prisoner; but join with
me in suffering for the gospel according to the power of GOD
who has SAVED us and has called us with a HOLY calling,
not according to our works, but according to HIS own purpose and grace which was granted us in Christ Jesus from
all eternity."* II Timothy 1:6-9

Today, the trip we three had planned for almost a year
began. My goals were many and my expectations high. My
main objective was to glorify Jesus in all that was to be
done. It is my desire that every step be directed by HIM!
(Proverbs 16:3)

In his book, *Conspiracy of Kindness,* Steve Sjogren made
a profound statement I want to remember every moment

1

of this mission trip. He said, "We do not have to have all of the answers a non-Christian might ask in order to make a significant impact on their life."

My first thought of what I hope to accomplish for Christ on this trip takes me back to a Sunday several years ago at COR. My wife, Cheri, and I went to hear Gregory Parr share his testimony. Parr, a former homeless person, had given his life to Christ as a result of our outreach free lunch program at Westport UMC. Every time he said "HOPE," we all responded, "JESUS!" These beautiful words ring with glorious harmony. When you hear and see "hope," you must say "Jesus." His testimony ended that day with another profound thought. Gregory said, "I just want to be of maximum service to my LORD Jesus." That is exactly what I feel as I sit in the Newark, New Jersey airport, waiting for the plane that will take me to Dusseldorf, Germany.

From Kansas City to Newark, I encouraged a flight attendant starved for Christian fellowship. I shared with her the challenging mission before me. I said, "This mission that awaits me is an astounding opportunity to experience Christianity at work in very difficult times and in very different surroundings. I pray that what I have witnessed on my former trips to Moscow has prepared me for what lies ahead." I told her that this trip would be a true test of my **total trust in HIM.** I am firmly convinced that every Christ-centered assignment we accept, no matter where the Lord may lead, results in our strength, faith and our witness for Christ becoming a mirror reflecting God's GLORY to all those around us. I told her for now, her mission field is right there on that aircraft. She has a wonderful opportunity to be a witness for Christ's love, grace and mercy to every difficult and grumpy person she encounters. A pleasant smile and a kind word on HIS behalf will go a long way to reach even the hardest heart. She said she had always dreamed of doing mission work for her church. She went on to say, "But I feel so inadequate. I don't feel 'called' or 'properly equipped' to do so." I read her our verse for today and I told her this, "Anyone who claims Jesus as LORD and SAVIOR has been called." I shared that, "God will never call us to do something for which he will not adequately equip us to accomplish for HIS sake and for HIS glory!"

Chuck Colson has so beautifully said, "God does not call the qualified but HE does qualify the called!"

As I sit here, I meditate on the last two mission trips to Russia. I remind myself of what I expressed to other team members who've never experienced a mission trip. My sermon to new mission volunteers is this, "Before you leave the United States, you will find your mind filled with a lot of STUFF. Stuff that will keep your thoughts cluttered and clogged with all kinds of things including your possessions from this world. These things will distract us from accomplishing GOD'S will and HIS purpose. After two or three days of totally saturating ourselves with HIS word and doing HIS work and being in close and constant contact with other people who love Jesus, we can truly stand on this great promise found in God's word for today: 'For He has not given us a spirit of fear, but of power, love and a sound mind.' The profound truth is this: When we give ourselves totally to serving others and when we surrender our every being to HIM and are totally committed to the work He has called us to do, all the 'STUFF' we brought with us on the mission trip will quickly disappear. You will find yourself witnessing and sharing Christ with such BOLDNESS and with such POWER that you won't even think it's you doing the witnessing! You will be able to recall Scripture verses in the Bible. NOW, all of a sudden, God's Word will come alive and you will quote Scriptures from memory! We can understand more clearly now what the Apostle Paul refers to, 'Giving us HIS Spirit **without fear**, but with **power, love** and a **sound mind**.'

"Please remember, FEAR all too often seems to be the cruel theme in our lives, the one thing that will keep us from doing and accomplishing what God has called us to do. You can proceed on HIS promise and move with confidence at HIS command. The truly miraculous is waiting for those who dare to take the LORD at HIS WORD, step out in faith and TRUST HIM!"

May I encourage you to take out your own Bible and take HIM at HIS word and read our verse for today with a new understanding? Let's look also at Jeremiah 33, verse 3, "Call to ME, and I will answer you, and I will tell you great and mighty things, which you do not know."

Tomorrow I will be in Germany at Jakob Lowen's home to begin the real mission. I pray that you will walk with me as we begin to build and then to cross the **BRIDGE INTO MISSION.**

DAY 2
Saturday, August 19, 2000

"Preach the word: be ready in season or out of season, reprove, rebuke, exhort, with great patience and instruction. For time will come when men will not endure sound doctrine: but wanting to have their ears tickled, they will accumulate for themselves teachers in accordance to their OWN desires! They will turn away from the truth and will turn to the myths of man." II Timothy 4:2-4

Saturday morning near the end of the 4956-mile flight, I looked out the window to see a magnificent sunrise at 36,000 feet. It reminds me of what it will be like as I open my eyes in Heaven and see the **"new light"** for the first time! The **Christ-light**, a sight so glorious it is beyond description! The plane was still and quiet. Many passengers were sleeping. I was certainly not one of them.

Willi met me at the airport. We flew right through customs and packed all of our "tools for JESUS" and suitcases in Willi's car. We were off! On to the famous Autobahn super highway!

Willi pointed out to me much beautiful scenery, but when traveling at 100 mph there is not much time to look around.

Let me tell you about the first member of our team, Wilhelm Dick. Boy, is he on fire for Jesus! He had spent the past month in Amsterdam at the "Billy Graham 2000 Pas-

5

tors Conference." Over 10,000 missionaries, pastors and evangelists were present, representing over 209 countries. The goal and main purpose was to train thousands of fellow believers in how to be more effective at winning our world for JESUS in their own countries.

We made a brief stop in the beautiful city of Cologne to visit the magnificent Dome of Cologne Cathedral. Begun in AD 314, it has been rebuilt many times and was finally completed in AD 1265. A few stone walls are all that is left of the original building. What a breathtaking church! The two things that really stood out were a solid gold crypt in the chancel area that may contain the relics and remains of the three Christmas Magi and a huge painting of Peter being crucified upside down as tradition tells us. Four watch towers surround this masterful structure called *Der Kölner Dom*. The Dom is 475 feet high, with 509 very narrow and dangerous steps for a 52-year-old man to negotiate. "Woody, everyone should climb them once!" Willi said.

As Willi and I continued on our 100 mph journey to Gummersbach, he shared with me the story of his family's persecution for being Christians. I'd always wondered how his people ended up in Siberia, as they were originally of German descent. His grandparents' family moved from Nazi Germany in 1937 to Omsk, Siberia, because his grandfather refused to serve in the army. Consequently, all of the men in this brave Mennonite family were sent to the Siberian death camps. It was not unusual for an entire family to live near the camps. While in this terrible place, Willi's grandfather prayed, "Lord, if you let me live, I will start the first evangelical church in Omsk, Siberia." The Lord heard and answered his prayer, and after only a year in prison he was released. In 1938, his church began its humble development. It operated continually even during the "Black Years," from 1929 until 1989. In 1987, during the first beginnings of restructuring *(Perestroika),* the church finally saw the end of the hate and cruelty of Communism. Willi said the reason this church was not destroyed during those difficult years was because most services were held in German, and the KGB did not really understand what was happening.

Around 1944, Stalin changed the entire course of Christianity in Russia with a new decree. Stalin personally recruited this new breed of henchmen and formed a group called "Lions of the Evangelical Church" Going into the very prisons where he had sent so many believers, he offered a deal to all who were imprisoned for religious reasons. Stalin said if the religious zealots would work for him and help him destroy all the evangelical churches in Russia, they would be freed. The goal and sole task was to destroy the thousands of small independent evangelical churches throughout the Soviet Union. Unfortunately, many turned their backs on God and gained release from the prisons of this world. These worst of all Judases informed the leaders of the "Lions of the Evangelical Church" movement where Christians were meeting and who was a true follower of Jesus. Stalin said, "These churches are considered to be 'subversive to the cause' and must be destroyed!" The task was accomplished by attempting to destroy the faith, hope and the sense of community built by these small groups of warriors for Jesus. Bibles were banned, church-sanctioned weddings were abolished, communion and baptisms were outlawed, and everything that meant "church" was stopped!

As the persecution grew, so did the true believers. They grew stronger and more determined than ever not to let anyone keep them from worshipping and serving the Lord. Many of these small bands of brave Christians formed an alliance. In 1960, the group organized themselves into a strong fellowship known as "Board of the Church." From their covenant and commitment to Christ, the Underground Evangelical Church was born. You will come to know two of the original leaders as this trip unfolds, Mikhail Ivanovich Khorev and Jakob Lowen.

Jakob Lowen is the "Rock of a Man" who gave our church the wonderful crystal chalice we began celebrating communion with on August 5-6. For many dark years, Jakob ran the underground printing press and was responsible for seeing that the outlawed Bible got into the homes of thousands of secret believers. The story of the crystal chalice will bring to light the respect and love that millions feel towards this great man of God.

In the former Soviet Republic of Latvia and the city of Valga, from 1960 until the end of the Soviet reign in 1990, several small evangelical churches worshiped the Lord Jesus in underground churches. They all knew that the punishment for the unlawful gatherings would be persecution: possibly torture and imprisonment far from their loved ones for many years. Despite the threats of the KGB and the local Communist authorities, the courageous believers met daily for Bible study, singing, worship, prayer and praise. The leader was Jakob Lowen. For thirty years he provided copies of one page of the Bible at a time, printed on his home-made printing press. This amazing press actually worked quite well using grape jelly for ink. Every week, a group of believers would be smuggled a page of God's Word, each in turn memorizing it and passing it on from house to house. These brave house churches observed Christ's HOLY Communion by taking turns in the celebration, using the priceless crystal chalice. This precious vessel was passed from church to church, and for over thirty years it represented the sacredness of Christ's Holy Communion.

When Communism fell and *Perestroika* began, the church leaders gave the hallowed vessel to the man who had constantly risked his life and his family's safety to enable thousands of spiritually hungry people to come to know Jesus as Lord and Savior. This piece of Soviet history is treasured by thousands of Russian-speaking Christians. Now this generous man has donated this vessel to all of us at COR.

Each time this marvelous vessel is consecrated for use in our communion services, we appreciate the lasting memories of sacrifice for our Lord that these brave believers endured.

May we never forget its HOLY purpose and those persecuted Christians who risked their very lives to continue this great and hallowed sacrament.

Most important is what it stands for. Remember what Christ said when HE told us, "This cup is the new covenant of my blood; as often as you drink it, do this in remembrance of ME."

Let me tell you a story about the man I will have the privilege to spend much time with once we arrive in Kishinev, Moldova. Mikhail Khorev, one of the brave founders of the Underground Evangelical Church, has served Christ openly and bravely for many years. For almost thirteen years, he was imprisoned for his uncompromising testimony for JESUS! This unbending man of God has written several books about his hellish confinement in the Russian Gulags. One book that unfortunately is no longer in print is appropriately titled, *Letters from a Soviet Prison*. In it, Mikhail vividly portrayed miraculous stories of his persecutions and triumphs over adversity. He tells the stories of sacrifices and heroic attempts of fellow believers to smuggle over 23 letters he wrote to his praying, patient family and church members. Mikhail is the father of Pavel Horev, who many may know as a Russian missionary in the Kansas City area. It should be noted that when Pavel came to America, he decided to change the spelling of his last name to match the correct pronunciation. Pavel dropped off the "K" and spells his last name "Horev." During one four-year prison term, Mikhail was sent to the prison camp in Omsk, Siberia. This is where, as children, Pavel and Willi met and began their life-long friendship. Another great leader of the underground church movement was

Georgi Vins. Many will remember his amazing release from prison from the worldwide headlines of April 27, 1979. Vins was halfway through a second ten-year prison term in a tortuous Soviet hard labor camp when he was miraculously whisked away, stripped of his Soviet citizenship, then exiled to the United States in a prisoners-for-spies exchange program under former President Jimmy Carter. Unaware of his destination, he was flown to Moscow with four other Soviet political dissidents. Still in his prison uniform with his long white beard, he was given an untailored dark suit of clothes and flown to New York. His wife and five children joined him in exile six weeks later, and Georgi Vins began to rebuild his life. His outspoken campaign to inform Americans of the terrible atrocities committed daily in these Gulag death camps led Georgi to Elkhart, Indiana, where he started a Christian publishing company. The *Prisoner Bulletin* publicized the plight of Christians in the Soviet Union, bringing a tremendous outcry from Christians the world over. Vins' *Bulletin* brought awareness to millions of believers and was instrumental in eventually improving the treatment of Christian prisoners in the Soviet Union. In 1988, after years of suffering and terrible persecution, it was reported that all the Christians had been freed. Georgi changed the name of his *Bulletin* to *The Russian Gospel Messenger.* In January 1998, this courageous warrior for Christ lost his battle for life but won the good fight of faith. Georgi Vins died of cancer in his adopted home of Elkhart, Indiana, at the age of 69. His untiring devotion to suffering believers all over the world and his many books will be remembered always.

The other leader of this movement spent 28 long years in many Soviet prison camps. Nicolae Chrapov wrote a best-selling book called, *The Happiness of a Lost Life.* For many years, these saintly men have been the subjects of numerous publications. These great men of God are yet a strong witness to the power of Christ's redeeming love.

After the fall of Communism in 1987-90, Jakob Lowen led several evangelical crusades right inside the walls of the Kremlin. Many Russian-speaking people know Jakob Lowen as "the friend to all men." Jakob told me that he was present when the infamous leader of the 1960s Cold-War, Nikita Khrushchev, accepted Christ as LORD! He also noted that before Boris Yeltsin's wife, Nina, died she accepted Christ as her SAVIOR!

DAY 3

Friday, August 20, 2000

"And we must proclaim Him, admonishing every man and teaching every man with all wisdom, that we may present every man complete in Christ. And for this purpose I labor, striving according to HIS power, which is at work mightily in me." Colossians 1:28-29

I woke at 6:00 a.m. Today is the Lord's Day. I prayed that the Lord would give me the words. My thoughts and objective are clear — to glorify HIM! I feel like the verse for today is very important and will be the foundation of the message that I bring. I want to tell the church about our work in Moscow and about the "Russian-American Initiative" that the United Methodist Church has begun.

I would guess that Jakob's church was more Mennonite than Baptist. About 90% of the congregation was families from the former Soviet Union that escaped Communism after World War II. I found the church building quite surprising! It was a brand-new structure with spotless marble floors and sparkling clean windows and freshly painted walls. The sanctuary on the main floor was not completed, so the congregation met in the fellowship hall downstairs. There were about a thousand people in the 800-chair facility. People didn't seem to mind that they had to stand. I wanted to take pictures, but felt it would be inappropriate

13

at the very formal two-hour service. Almost all the men wore coats and ties. All the married women sat, heads covered, on one side of the church. Their coverings consisted of a carefully folded colorful scarf. The children all came up to the front, sitting still and listening quietly and amazingly attentive. I enjoyed studying the people and noticed them watching me, especially the little ones. I do not know how they knew I was an American, but they knew! I smiled at them and they would look away, blushing and giggling. Several men shared the pulpit for the usual things. Jakob's wife gave the children's sermon. Several men spoke in a combination German, Russian dialect that Willi said is very difficult to understand, let alone interpret.

As I was introduced I felt so humbled and privileged to greet these people and represent the United Methodist Church of the Resurrection from Leawood, Kansas, AMERICA! I shared greetings and told the congregation what an honor it was to call Jakob Lowen my friend. I shared how the Lord had brought Cheri and me into a ministry with the wonderful Russian-speaking people. I told of how our church had a vision of marvelous things we could do after our pastor Adam Hamilton returned from his first trip to Moscow in 1995.

I really felt like I was in a church service in Russia. There were many older women and men, all with the same expressions, and all the women seemed to be dressed alike. They really seemed to get excited and even smiled a little when I talked about our work and our love for the Russian-speaking people. Then I addressed the children who were listening very attentively. I told them I had brought each one of them a very special gift all the way from America. I said that our Sunday school classes had made something **just for them**. I wanted to capture this moment forever! Those precious little faces lit up and grinned from ear to ear. I held one of the "Gospel bracelets" up high so all of them could see. Then, very slowly, going through all of the different colored beads, I told them the salvation story of Jesus, describing each color and what it meant. I encouraged them to be bold with these "witnessing tools." I said, "Tell all of your friends and your family members who do not come to church what Jesus has done for each one of them." I told them each person who received a "Gospel bracelet" could become a "little missionary for Jesus!" With great joy I expressed to them that after the service, they could come up to me and I would personally equip every one of them with one of these great "jewels of the faith."

Willi brought the main message, speaking on Isaiah 55. He told the people about the sovereignty and the majesty of God and gave a great story of hope and loving your brother.

The church service ended two hours later, but not before they did something I'd never seen. Spontaneous prayer and praise was received from anyone who felt led. Not like some of the churches that I have been where it seemed too many people were trying to bring attention to themselves. This church was bringing praise and adoration to our LORD! Some just murmured a short word, others spoke a phrase or verse of Scripture, and some prayed boldly, others quietly. What a witness of beautiful worship and the spontaneous moving of the Holy Spirit!

When all were finished, Willi gave a simple, "AH-MEEN!" (AMEN)

Then I discovered one of the reasons the Lord sent me on this trip! One-hundred sixty-three little people came rushing up to me and formed a massive line, happy as Christmas morning kids. They all had huge smiles and each one held out their precious little hands to receive their gift from the generous Americans from the Kansas City area. I personally placed each bracelet on every one of those precious little children. As I adjusted the leather thong to fit each wrist, I looked into their beautiful innocent eyes and said, "Jesus loves you so much!" They showed such trust, such innocence, such compassion! I was so overwhelmed by this act of worship that I began to cry.

This worship experience brought a vivid picture to my mind: how Jesus loved the little children, how they came to HIM in total trust. I saw in my mind, this is just how HE wants us all to come to HIM, holding our arms wide open to receive HIS compassion and love. I gave these children a small gift, but Jesus gives us the most unbelievable gift imaginable, ETERNAL LIFE! If nothing else happens on this trip, these "jewels of the faith" given in HIS love have paid royal dividends into HIS eternal kingdom!

We returned to Jakob's house for lunch, or I should say, feast. For the rest of the afternoon it was church at home, singing songs until time to eat. Then I realized, on Sunday the meal lasts all afternoon. I am amazed at how much food Jakob's wife, Irma, can prepare on such a small cook top and with no microwave either!

It was refreshing to see people not in a hurry, laughing and having such fun by just being together. Six of Jakob's twelve children — YES, I did say twelve, joined us for the afternoon along with Willi and his brother Victor, his wife and three children. Jakob's saintly wife, Irma, prepares three meals a day for anywhere from 6 to 60. No one worries that the dishes don't match or a fork is bent or the drinking glasses might be empty jelly jars. I cannot remember the last time I spent an entire Sunday in total rest, surrounded by so many joyous and praise-filled people. All of Jakob's children are accomplished musicians. It was wonderful to sit and listen to Willi play the violin and Victor, the piano. Jakob's children are a choir within themselves. I cannot help but think of the Von Trapp family singers in *The Sound of Music*. Yes, they sang "Edelweiss" — in perfect five-part harmony! I know from now until the Lord takes me home, every time I hear "Edelweiss," I will think of this day.

These wonderful Christ-centered people gave me the privilege of experiencing a living picture of what it is like

The beautiful Lowen children (young adults) that are still living at home with Jakob and Irma.

to become adopted into a family of GOD. I told Jakob seeing his family living totally for Christ reminds me of what the Apostle Paul was saying to us in Romans 8:15, "For you have not received the spirit of slavery leading to fear again, but you have received a spirit of **adoption** as sons by which we cry out, 'ABBA! FATHER!'" I see Jakob, just like our Heavenly Father, as a perfect description of what this verse is interpreted to mean; Abba Father — an unconditionally loving father full of mercy and grace.

I asked Lisa if she missed television, and her reply fits this family very appropriately. She said, "Woody, living in a house with 12 kids, a preacher and a preacher's wife, who needs any additional entertainment?"

After the first tasting meal, all the kids pitched in to clean up. While they were cleaning up, Irma sat down for the first time in two days! This wonderful woman of God was actually sitting in a chair while the nine grandchildren were taking turns enjoying sitting in her love-filled lap.

Jakob boldly proclaimed for all to hear, **"In honor of our American guest, it is now time for the serious meal!"** Jakob built a big fire in their homemade brick fire pit, and the fun continued for the rest of the afternoon and well into the evening. The feast consisted of a series of old - fashioned American BBQ style foods. For the rest of the afternoon and well into the evening we grazed and gorged ourselves. Many people from the church stopped by to say hi or to sing and, of course, there was plenty of good food to eat. What a joyous lifestyle that we should take note of. This was truly the Lord's Day! We did rejoice and were exceedingly glad in it! I know it probably won't be possible, but may I strive to bring this wonderfully simple way of living back with me and introduce it to my family!

DAY 4

Monday, August 21, 2000

"And the Lord said to Paul in the night by a vision, "Do not be afraid any longer, but go on speaking and do not be silent; I am with you, and no man will attack you to harm you, for I have many people in the city." Acts 18:9-10

Here I am at ORA headquarters! (Operation Reach All, www.orainternational.org) Boy, is this exciting! I just recorded a message that will be broadcast over *Far East Broadcasting Network* to more than 10 million people! The broadcast will go to Saipan, Great Britain, Ecuador and Africa. The message would have gone to 40 million, but just last month they had to eliminate all of Russia because of financial reasons. All communication will be translated into the Russian language. I will give more information tonight about this great outreach. While on the air, I shared how COR was called to work with the Russian-speaking people. I spoke for about 10 minutes on how the vision first began. I spoke of Adam's first visit to Moscow in 1995, and followed with the story of our first church-wide Moscow mission trip in 1997. I then told of the 1998 *Russian-American Leadership Institute* that was held in Kansas City, our second mission trip to Moscow in 1999 and finally, the current 2000 *Russian-American Institute*. I ended my speech with the story of the new journey that I will be challenged to begin tomorrow in Kishinev, Moldova.

I am saddened because our travel plans for the mission trip have been changed. Willi has been quite ill since he came back from his exhausting trip to Amsterdam. He does not feel able to make the trip as originally planned by automobile. Now I will fly to Kishinev, Moldova, by myself, facing the customs officials without an interpreter. Pavel told me to be sure to claim everything that I am bringing or they will probably take it! Pray that I won't forget a thing! Pavel will pick me up at the airport, but first I have to clear customs — all by myself? Woody is the guy who gets lost in his own backyard! So far, this is the only thing that brings me any concern.

Once in Kishinev, Pavel said we would travel by auto to many small cities and villages nearby. He has made arrangements for us to share the LORD in orphanages, state-run hospitals, nursing facilities and possibly some prisons. I am very sorry that we did not get to travel across all of the different countries as we had originally planned, but this is the Lord's trip, and who am I to be disappointed because my plans were changed!

Let me add a bit more information about the radio station. Jakob's next to the oldest son, Victor, is in charge of all of the broadcasting and directing. This station transmits entirely Christian broadcasting messages via short wave over the *Far East Broadcasting Network*. Listeners and private ministries support it. All Russian programs are mostly built upon Jakob's teaching the Bible — verse by verse and book by book. Monday is children's themes. Tuesday is Biblical training for adults. Wednesday is Jakob's day for reading listeners' questions and then giving answers. It is also prayer request day. Thursday is again adult teaching, and Friday is geared to young adults. All day Saturday is children's day again, and Sundays are dedicated to pre-recorded preaching services that Jakob has proclaimed from all over the world.

Jakob's heart was broken last month when ORA had to eliminate the broadcasts over the Russian airways. Each station should be self-supporting after six months. The Russian-speaking people in the former Soviet Union are so poor they could not give enough to support the $35 per day it costs to reach 30 million radio listeners. Thirty-five dollars per day to reach 30 million people with solid Bible teaching programs and wonderful encouragement from a man that so many Russian-speaking people respect and love so dearly! I do not know how much $35 a day divided by 30 million is, but it is a very small investment that has paid a huge spiritual dividend!

The ministry of ORA does, however, send out over 250,000 of Jakob's quarterly newsletters called *NEW FIELDS* into many areas of the former Soviet Union. These newsletters contain articles of current information on the movement and mission work of ORA, as well as highlights and outlines from his radio broadcasts. Jakob's devoted crusaders read and re-read each publication. It will be passed on for a long time to come to many different homes as well as small struggling "cell churches." For thousands of spiritually hungry souls this publication is the only Christian literature they receive.

It soon becomes easy to see and understand the far-reaching love that these people have for this great man of GOD, Jakob Lowen. Cheri and I had the wonderful privilege of getting to know him quite well when he stayed in our home for several days. He totally won our hearts at this first uniting of spirits and ideas in November 1999. He had come to America to help Pavel and Willi start a new ministry. This wonderful endeavor, which incidentally was named after Jakob's publications, is called *New Fields World Wide Ministry, Inc.* Their mission is to work with newly immigrated Russian-speaking people in the Kansas City area. Most of the time when these new hungry-to-be-Americans arrive, they have only the clothes on their backs. Pavel and

Willi will help these precious poor people get enrolled in English classes, find jobs and get decent housing. Helping them get established with the basic essentials for a new chance and a new beginning here in GOD BLESS AMERICA is Pavel and Willi's calling and purpose. Most importantly, these new and very hard-working folks quickly get involved with other Russian-speaking Christians in fellowship and worship experiences.

We left the radio station and Jakob drove me around the city of Gummersbach. Here is my very limited impression of Germany. It is very clean and free from litter and trash. The people that I met seem to take great pride in their country. Their homes and cars and the things they own are well maintained. All buildings look freshly painted with sparkling clean windows. I was truly honored and humbled by the respect that I was shown while visiting this beautiful, picturesque city.

Jakob took me to see a man named Victor Paplov, a wonderful musician who has been through some very hard times in the past two years. Somehow he got involved with the Russian Mafia. He has been hunted for several years and almost caught and killed numerous times. He and his family escaped from the former Soviet Republic and came to Gummersbach. He knew that Jakob Lowen was there, "the friend to all people." The Russian Mafia, referred to by the locals as the *Nuva-Ruska,* followed his trail and found out where he was staying. Three thugs came to Jakob's house with guns and told Jakob that if he did not tell them where Victor was they would kill him. They pushed themselves inside Jakob's home. Jakob told them they could kill him if they wanted to but he would never tell them where Victor was. Then Jakob began to pray in a very loud Russian voice for salvation for these men. He prayed that God would move in their hearts to let them see that Victor was a good man and that he did not cheat anyone. The leader of the group told the others, "We are finished here. The man we are looking for is dead." They left without finding Victor, and Jakob said, "The Lord went before me, HE is my strength and my shield!" Deuteronomy 31:6, assures us, "Be strong and courageous, do not be afraid or tremble at them, for the LORD your GOD is the one who goes with you, HE will not fail you or forsake you!" Go back and read our verse for today.

The people in this town of 63,000 seem to be afraid of Victor. No one will hire him to work within his field of music. His desire is to lead choirs or teach singing or do anything that relates to church work. Since he is unable to accomplish this, he survives by doing handyman work or clean-up wherever he can. I do not understand all the details surrounding this man, but Jakob tries to help him by keeping him busy around the church.

I was truly blessed as Victor sang, played piano and then guitar for me. He gave me a tape of his Christian music that was recorded at the ORA radio station. Most of the songs on the tape are songs he wrote while in the Russian army. The songs are stories of the persecutions he endured being a Christian during the very difficult days of Communism. Before I left, I prayed with him. I gave him some money from the church that will enable him to buy some food and some clothes for his children before this year's school term starts.

When we arrived back at Jakob's home, I was very surprised and quite humbled that this wonderful family had planned a going-away party for me. I was blessed by getting to meet 11 of the 12 children. Now I have met all but Katya, who lives in the United States.

The final evening with this blessed family, Irma (Jakob calls her appropriately, "My wife with angel wings") fixed dinner for 17 adults and nine grandchildren. What a tribe! What a rich blessing for me! I have never seen so many people in one immediate family all gathered together in one house and all at the same time. Some of his children drove as far as a hundred miles to see me.

Jakob Lowen and his wonderful Christ-centered family as we celebrated our last full day together.

After dinner, Jakob asked me to tell his clan about how I was called to work with the Russian-speaking people. I shared with them the vision and the involvement and the calling that our church responded to after Adam returned from his first trip to Moscow in 1995. I told them how this trip was going to be different, because of where we would be going and the work we would be doing for the Lord. We were all startled when one of Jakob's daughters started to chuckle. Jakob asked her to tell us all what was so funny. Lillia laughed and said, "I was talking to one of my dear friends who lives in Kishinev, and she said that next week an American missionary was coming to preach in their town." Lillia said, "Woody, you must be the one!"

My pride sometimes has a tendency to get in the way of the Lord's work, and this was certainly one of those times. I had to step back and quote John 3:30, "I must decrease and HE must increase."

We sang songs and praised the Lord until well after 10 p.m. I equipped all the grandchildren with Gospel bracelets and the little Jesus loves you stickers. I also gave them plenty of Gospel bracelets to give out at next week's worship services.

After the infantry had gone home, I presented Irma and Jakob with one of the Waterford Crystal crosses that the Irish Crystal Company of Overland Park, Kansas had donated for me to give as house gifts. Irma said she did not deserve such a gift of fine beauty. I assured her that after seeing what she had done today and all week long, when the Lord calls her home and she gets to glory, HE is going to say, "IRMA, you come over here and sit next to me!" She and Jakob laughed, and we ended the evening on our knees in a prayer of thanksgiving and praise.

DAY 5

Tuesday, August 22, 2000

"And HE said to all of them, "Go into all of the world and preach the gospel to all creation. He who has believed and is baptized shall be saved. And these signs will accompany those who have believed: in My name they will cast out demons, they will speak with a new tongue; they will pick up serpents, and if they drink any deadly poison, it shall not hurt them; they will lay hands on the sick and they will recover." Mark 16:15-18

Because I had to leave this wonderful Christ-filled home, I arose very early this morning to interview Irma. I wanted to learn about her childhood and how she came to Jesus and how she and Jakob had met.

Irma was born in a small village in central Russia. Her father was killed in World War II when she was only three. The year after her father was killed, her mother died when a tree fell on her. Irma, a sister and a brother went to live with their elderly grandparents. Two years later, the grandfather died, leaving only the grandmother to raise the three children. They were so poor that all Irma remembers about growing up was going to bed hungry every night. Her diet consisted mostly of potatoes and bread and what vegetables they could grow in the terrible rocky, dry, arid soil. Irma said when she was 13 an uncle sold his only suit to get enough money to bring the children to live with him in Kazatstan. As a child, she does not remember much about worship experiences. She remembers going to the Russian Orthodox Church several times. She told me she never knew what all the chanting and rocking back and forth was all about, but it did scare her. As a young and impressionable child, her first thoughts about God were that HE was hard, cruel, cold and uncaring.

Her first encounter with the living LORD came when she was 16. Irma said on Sundays she would walk to a village by a large prison. There she would listen to a very brave warrior for Christ named Stapan DuBovoy. Stapan was imprisoned for his testimony for Christ for a total of 28 years. Irma went on to explain that the prison officials would let the prisoners outside for two hours each week. This brave man chose to use his precious freedom time to preach to the outside world during his brief fresh-air break. He would stand as close to the high fence as he could and call people to repentance with the boldness of Peter. Let us examine the Biblical account that closely parallels this story. Peter said in Acts 5:29, "But Peter and the apostles told the officials and the high priests, "We must obey God rather than man — and they kept on preaching."

This great warrior for Christ is still alive and preaching each day at the age of 90. His son lives in Kishinev, so I hope to see him while I am there.

Jakob and Irma met when she was 17 and he was 18. One day, Irma asked Jakob to go with her to hear Stapan DeBovoy preach at the prison fence. After several weeks of resisting he finally went.

Jakob gave his life to Christ the year after they were married. For the next seven years, all he did when he was not working in the iron mines deep beneath the outside world was read his Bible and memorize scripture.

Jakob's first Bible is quite a story in itself. When he was a young boy, the KGB came and took his uncle away to Siberia for teaching and preaching "treasonous things against the government." When his uncle knew the KGB agents were about to arrest him, he gave his precious Bible to Jakob. The brave uncle said to Jakob, "Boy, no matter what happens to me or what might happen to you, do not let the **Word of God** be taken by the KGB! You must protect God's Word with your life! If they come and get you too, you must pass it on to someone else who needs these words and who will protect it from being destroyed."

I asked him if he still had this Bible and he and Irma began to laugh! Jakob looked at me and said one of his favorite English phrases, "Woody, it is not possible!" Then he went on to say, when he was not involved in Bible study and his scripture memorization, he would hide God's Word in a safe place he had made. Several times, at any hour of the day or night, the KGB paid Jakob surprise visits. Their goal was to try and catch him in the treasonous act of reading a Bible, which, by the way, was punishable by up to four years in prison!

I must tell you what actually happened to this very special Bible. Jakob said, "Woody, my hiding place was not so good of one." He and Irma chuckled and then he finished, "The rats in the house liked paper and they ate my Bible." I asked him if the rats preferred the Old Testament or the New Testament? He replied with much laughter, "Woody, the rats are about as dumb as the Russian KGB. I don't think they could read very well!"

Jakob's brave uncle who had given this very special Bible to him died in prison. Jakob said one of his great joys as a young man was to visit him in prison before he went on to be with Jesus. Jakob was able to tell him in his own Christian codes that he, too, had given his life to Christ. His uncle told him something that changed Jakob's life forever. "Jakob, there is an all-out war going on now. This evil government wants to destroy all Christians. You must be prepared at all times to preach and to tell others about Jesus; be brave and bold. Never give up and never turn against a brother in Christ!"

Jakob told me that morning, "Most preachers are called by God to preach the Gospel. But I guess I was first called and told by my uncle." Jakob's uncle told him on that last visit to the prison, "Very soon I am going to get to see Jesus and how wonderful that day is going to be. You must tell others about Jesus!"

In 1960, the Lowen family moved to Volga, Latvia. They were very poor and now had six small children. It was in Latvia that Jakob and several other brave believers formed the group called the Board of the Underground Church, which was the basis for today's Evangelical Christian Baptist Church. Still today, Jakob Lowen and all of Pavel Horev's family preach the same message and live by the same doctrine they helped establish many years ago. Since the original formation, many other similar church affiliations have been founded across the world.

Jakob soon began operating his black market Bible printing press. The KGB knew that many people in the area were involved with this so-called subversive group and **someone** had access to a printing press. So it was all-out war to find the leaders of this band of rebels and bring them to punishment. This amazing printing press was, at that time, the only one of its kind. Jakob said, "GOD's printing press was miraculously designed to be able to print on both sides of the paper at once!" It was made out of a washing machine and bicycle parts and could be torn down in less than three minutes. It would fit in a couple of shopping bags and could be carried anywhere. They used grape jelly for ink. Jakob told me that they had to move their operation every day. They had their own code and words for protection from any inside traitors. Jakob finally decided that the safest place for the printing press was a place where the KGB would never think to look. So one day they moved their operation and all of their supplies, along with a couple dozen hungry pigs into a room right under the headquarters of the KGB. During the day, they would not feed the pigs anything, so at night they would make plenty of horribly loud squealing and grunting noises while they were rooting around and eating everything in sight. These unfamiliar sounds were loud enough to cover up the thrashing noise of the printing press as it pounded out another page of God's Word.

I asked Irma what was the most moving testimony of the power and miracles of Christ that she had ever personally witnessed. She said, "Woody, many people in our town were depending upon us as well as our six small children. We were very poor, but after working all night long on the printing press, the workers were very hungry. There was no food, so I asked Jakob, "What can we do?" and Jakob said, "Irma, we must pray and believe." Irma looked all around the tiny kitchen and found a half empty (or half full, depending upon your frame of mind) box of some kind of mustard seed. She took a few seeds out of the box and made a small pot of what she thought was to be a tasteless soup. She told of how God turned this blessed brew into a wonderful pot of very tasty stew! The miracle of the five loaves and the two fishes in Matthew 14 came to life. That night and the following nights for over a month she took the same number of seeds and put them in the same pot and made the same soup, and every night with the same miraculous results. They all ate their fill and were not hungry, but there was nothing wasted.

I asked Jakob what was the most amazing and profound miracle that he had ever witnessed. He said, "One time I was very, very ill and my family and friends forced me to go to the doctor. The doctors of the hospital in the town in which we were living were allied with the KGB and could not be trusted. I accidentally overheard them saying that they were going to give me an injection that would kill me instantly. Then I told God, 'God, here is your humble servant. Do you want me to come home now or is there still work for me to do here? But God, whatever you want is okay with me.'" He said that all of a sudden he became very warm and drowsy, the way the anesthesia makes you feel just before you go under the knife for an operation. The only problem was, they had not given him the injection yet. Jakob said he had total peace, and he knew that our sovereign God was in absolute control, no matter what the outcome. The two doctors and three nurses came into the room and told him he had better sit down for this shot, so he did. They gave him his special booster and waited a minute for its deadly serum to take its toll. Finally Jakob broke this very unusual silence by stating, "I am feeling much better now — may I go home?" While the five of them just stood there stunned and speechless, this dead man put on his clothes and walked home. Not only was he ALIVE, but he was now totally healed of his pneumonia. Again, why don't you stop and read this amazing story almost word for word from your own Bible in Mark 16:15-18.

This ends my stay with a truly remarkable family. God has anointed and used this family in ways that we cannot even imagine or comprehend! Jakob Lowen is working on his fifth book. He said that when it is completed, and if the Lord allows, he would think about writing an autobiography. Jakob's true life story will touch millions of lives and encourage many Christians who are suffering persecution today to keep the faith. In II Timothy 4:7, we read, "I have fought a good fight, I have finished the course, I have kept the faith." This is truly Jakob Lowen's legacy!

The drive to the airport in Frankfurt took about two hours. Peter Rempel drove me. He is Jakob's assistant at the radio station and also his associate pastor. This great man of God has a very quiet disposition and reminds me so much of my dear brother in Christ, Konstantin Vaganov. I hope to see Konstantin next week in Moscow. Peter exhibited today, by being so helpful to me, the gift of serving and mercy. After he helped me get checked in with the airline for my two-hour flight to Kishinev, Moldova, we sat down to visit over a cup of coffee. A young man with a dark complexion came up to us and asked me a question about a particular airline. He spoke perfect English, so I thought maybe he was Canadian. He saw my "I Am Loved" pin and asked where I was going and if I spoke Russian. I told him all about the mission trip, and we began a very interesting discussion about Jesus. I boldly told him the pin meant that **I was loved by Christ**! I shared with him what JESUS had done in my life and how HE had changed me completely. I felt the powerful presence of the Holy Spirit. God's Spirit surrounded us as we visited. This young man was so open, so hungry and eager to ask questions about the Bible and about how to know Christ!

To my surprise, he was from the eastern Russian area called Uzbekistan. He told me he was raised a Moslem, but he really did not believe in anything. I asked him if he believed that it was just chance that out of 10,000 people in this huge airport that he just happened upon me? Then I asked him if maybe there were some deep questions that he had been asking about God's very existence? I said to him, "If there is a God and Jesus was the Messiah, do you want to know more about HIM?" I was not surprised when he said, "Yes! I have really been searching and I thought that maybe I had found God just a week ago. I encountered some young Mormon missionaries." He continued, "I listened carefully to them and I even read their literature, but they sounded more like they were trying to get me to join their group than to help me to find and learn about God." I then told him that I felt God had truly answered his prayers this very day! There was no way we were just meeting by chance. God had ordained this meeting! I read to him a couple of verses in the Bible about how God will send someone who knows the truth to cross the path of someone who is searching for the real truth. In Proverbs 8:17, God says, **"I love** those who love me: and those who will diligently seek me will find me"! Then I read to him Jeremiah 29:12-13, **"Then you will call upon ME and come and pray to ME and I will listen to you. And you will seek ME and find ME, when you search for ME with all of your heart."**

I pulled out the *4-spiritual laws* in Russian and gave him several copies. I told him that every question he has ever asked about a loving and caring God could be answered completely by just reading this tiny booklet. I assured him that after reading it and understanding the truths contained in this small pamphlet, he should then be honest and just say, "God, if this strange man in the airport is telling me TRUTH, then make it known to me."

I inquired if he owned a Christian Bible. He startled me when he said that it was illegal to have this type of book in his country. But he said that he would give anything to receive one! I told him that I would try to get a Bible to him through the mail, but there is no guarantee that he would receive it. He pleaded for me to please try! It was such a shame that I did not have one of the 6,500 Russian language Bibles COR purchased for us to hand out. Please pray for this young man named Deanise.

Isn't God wonderful??????!!!!!!!!!!!! Here is a guy, out of the blue, far from his own very anti-Christian country on a holiday asking sincere and searching questions about God. Lo and behold, I get to be an instrument of God's love. What a privilege to be sent there just for this young man! Look at I Peter 3:15, "But sanctify Christ in your heart, always being ready to make a defense to every one who asks you to give an account for the hope that is in you, yet with gentleness and reverence." Please pray that he will see Christ as LORD and invite HIM into his heart.

I boarded the plane with no problem at all. When I landed in Kishinev, there was no one at the visa application desk and no one spoke a word of the King's English! I waited for about an hour in this terribly hot airport, and I must tell you, I was getting a little nervous. Finally, Pavel showed up to rescue me. Thankfully, he knew someone who let him cross over the custom and immigration section. Boy, was I glad to see him!

We had about a 30-minute drive back to the 50-year-old apartment building where Pavel has lived for 27 years of his life. Most all of these tiny flats, as they are called, have a very small kitchen, one bathroom, only one bedroom and a couch-bed that Pavel had to share while he was growing up with two brothers. These flats all look the same and they all have the same furnishings. Pavel's elderly mother and very sick father live on the fifth floor. There is no working elevator in this old, terribly run-down building. I was not surprised to find things in the shape that they were in.

Most areas of Moscow have benefitted greatly from the fall of Communism. Today, 10 years later, other republics of the former Soviet Union are in shambles. The reason has become obvious to me. The day Communism fell, the people found themselves instantly cut off from sending their goods and food products into the two major cities, Moscow and St. Petersburg. They have been literally choked off and left with no support and no funding to provide anything for themselves. The government is bankrupt. Everything is in an awful state of deterioration. Corruption is rampant. To make matters worse, if that is possible, there has been no rain for two months and all the crops are dead. There is no industry and no jobs. The people who work for the state continue to work without any pay, because if they quit they will lose their small pension check of about $7 per month.

Let me tell you a little bit about the country of Moldova. Moldova is commonly called "the land in the middle" because it is tucked between the two much larger countries it borders. Romania follows from the north all the way to the south along the western side, and the huge country of the Ukraine to its north and all the way to the south on the

Pavel watching the local "cow" traffic on a typical side road in Kishinev. Note the occupied but uncompleted homes that have been this way since the fall of Communism in 1989.

eastern borders. The population of Moldova is about 4,500,000. The largest city is the capital city, Kishinev. Kishinev has a population of about 800,000. The local people refer their capital city as "Chisinau." There are over 29 different ethno-linguistic groups. Sixty-six percent of them claim to be members of the Russian Orthodox Church, but many of these attend church less than once a year. Since this country in not part of Russia any more, the Orthodox sister churches in Moldova are now called the Romanian Orthodox. The breakdown of the other religious groups officially registered with the government are: 2.5% Catholic, 1.7% Protestant, 1.5% Jewish. Twenty-nine percent consider themselves to be non-religious and atheist. The official language is now Romanian, ending the 70-year span during which the Soviets demanded Russian be taught and spoken. But all the time I was there, I never heard anyone speaking Romanian. From 1924 until 1989, Moldova was swallowed up by the voracious greed of the Soviet Union. Those 65 years of domination remain evident today by this new country's dire economic situation. In August 1991, the new government declared its independence from the Soviets and a new constitution was established. Moldova became an independent republic with its own parliament. In 1994, the people of Moldova established their own currency, the *Lei,* abandoning the Soviet-imposed Russian ruble.

It is evident that the people of Moldova are in much worse shape now than many other areas of the former Soviet Union. There were many houses being built before the fall of Communism. After *Perestroika* occurred, the construction instantly stopped. Now, almost 10 years later, the people have finally completed maybe only one room of a fairly large house. You drive by and you see a nice-sized block or stone home under construction, and there is only one room that is finished! So the entire family lives in this part of the uncompleted dwelling. Many people are living in homes that do not have a permanent roof on them. If you should have to leave your uncompleted home unattended for over a day, when you returned there would be nothing there. Your desperate neighbors will have taken every piece of rebar that is not totally covered by cement. They will also have taken every piece of copper and aluminum out of the building. Even the loose building stones will have been hauled away.

Things are so bad that the people have lost all hope, that is, unless they have trusted Christ as Lord. Christ's love for us is not dependent on our prosperity. Christ's love for us is unconditional and never ending! Even in these horrible circumstances, He is still Lord. The Christians here are a very strong close-knit band of unbelievably helping people. Their lifestyles are much like that of our Amish and

Mennonite brothers and sisters in Christ. This is one of the reasons that the Mennonite churches offer so much support to these strong and resilient people.

There are people everywhere selling anything that they own in order to get a little money to buy bread and some milk. If they have two pairs of shoes, they will sell one. The streets are lined with lonely and helpless people looking for a way to survive. This is why crime is so bad. You do not dare leave your flat unlocked for a second or you will be targeted for a break-in. Pavel was very worried about taking my suitcases out of the car in the light. Even in the terrible heat, you cannot keep your windows open unless you have steel bars on them.

As soon as we arrived, thankfully without any incidents, we took our things from the car. This very special vehicle was an answer to prayer. One of Pavel's dear brothers in the Lord had graciously loaned the car to us for the entire mission. Praise the Lord!!!

Pavel's cousin, Daniel Apostu, is letting me stay at his flat. The wonderful news is that this will be my home during the entire time I am in Moldova! Halleluiah, Praise His Name! A quiet place in which to retire after an exhausting day in ministry. Daniel said that while I was there, he would stay at his experimental farm outside town. Daniel's flat is in the same complex as Pavel's mom and dad's, so I do not have far to yell for HELP!

Maybe that was a bad choice of words?

After we met and then visited a bit with Daniel and his fiancée, Veroica, we went up to the Khorevs' flat. What a joy to finally get to meet his mom and dad. Pavel's brother, Ivan, was waiting there with his eight children to greet us. These precious little ones all came to life when I got out my bag of goodies. I equipped them from head to toe with the whole works. They quickly became friends with this strange-talking man from America.

Pavel's father, Mikhail, is 69 and is in very poor health.

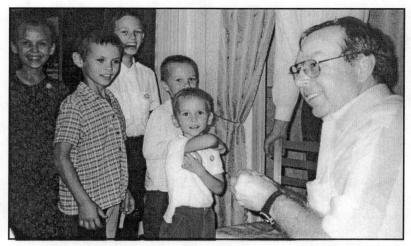

Pavel's brother, Pastor Ivan Khorev, with his eight children receiving their "goodies" from the strange-talking man from Kansas City.

He has only 2% vision in one eye and not much better in the other. He also has a terribly painful and horrible sounding cough. I would guess that he has pneumonia. His legs and feet are so swollen that he cannot wear trousers and of course, no shoes. His legs are in this terrible condition because they were frozen when he was placed in a ghastly solitary confinement cell while in prison. One of his legs has gangrene and needs to be amputated. Actually, I thought that this surgery had already been done, but it has not. You see, to have this kind of major surgery, one would have to provide his own morphine, syringes, bandages, antibiotics, gauze and all the necessary surgical wrappings. You would also need to have enough money to pay for your stay in the hospital. There is no money! Pavel sends every dime he can to help them, but it seems all the things they need for this surgery will have to be purchased on the black market. Pavel and his family are strictly opposed to dealings of any kind with these people. They don't know at this time when the surgery can be done. Just think about it, and we complain about the food in our hospitals?

The story behind this remarkable man's bravery while he was in solitary confinement cell is a testimony to the power and the mercy of Christ. Pavel's father spent almost 13 years of his life in Siberian prison camps. He was found guilty and sentenced for these terribly perilous crimes:

1. Helping others within the church by promoting Bible reading and preaching Jesus, HIS forgiveness and HIS love.
2. Organizing and distributing forbidden Christian literature to orphan children.
3. Holding public baptisms and promoting Christian marriages within the church.

In 1984, while serving his last prison term of four years, Mikhail was sent into solitary confinement for 25 days for preaching and quoting scriptures out loud. The cruel prison guards sent him to HELL in a cell that was 6 x 6 x 5 feet high. He could not stand erect in this horrible place of constant suffering. There was **no heat** and it was in the middle of one of Siberia's worst winters. Positioned all over the floor, inside this torturous cell, were 6-inch-high steel spikes sunk into the cement pointing upwards and placed ten inches apart. You could step but there was no way one could sit or lie down. Most people went mad and just fell on the spikes and welcomed death after two or three days, but not this great man of God! He somehow positioned his body to lean against the wall and slept in this painful position. Mikhail Khorev is the saint of all saints. This man has been persecuted more for his faith in Christ than any of us can even imagine. During this heinous 25-day sentence, "man's purpose was for him to die, but God's purpose was for him to exhibit the power of prayer and to display the extent of God's immeasurable grace and mercy. This horrible solitary confinement cell was given the name Africancan, because if you did survive for the normal sentencing of two or three terrible and torturous days, you would be carried out totally blackened from all the bruising of the spikes. It is believed that the jailors who watched over him ended up giving their lives to Christ some time later. These two jailors knew of Mikhail's strong faith, so they found this watch particularly interesting. They would listen at the door, but all they heard was singing and great shouts of praise! This powerful man of God was praying out loud for all of his family and the other persecuted prisoners. Behold, he was even praying for the people who put him in this place of constant agony and torture. When he wasn't praying, he would recite scripture and sing hymns of worship and songs of praise to the great author of all mercy and grace.

The Lord gave Mikhail special strength and that special peace to endure this HELL for those horrifying days. When the sentence was completed, the two curious jailors slowly opened the door. If this brave man was still alive, they expected him to be clinging to only an ounce of life. They stepped into this HOLE in HELL to carry him out. But there, before them, was a witness of a true miracle! A miracle that only could be attributed to a faithful and merciful GOD! This man, full of the peace that passes all human comprehension walked out on his own singing praises to our LORD. The jailors said, "This man is from God if he is not a god."

This amazing story reminds me of the Apostle Paul's exhortations in Colossians 3:15-17, "And let the peace of Christ rule in your hearts, to which indeed you were called in one body; and be thankful. Let the WORD of CHRIST richly dwell within you; with all wisdom teaching and admonishing one another with psalms and hymns and spiritual songs, singing with thankfulness in your hearts to GOD! And whatever you do in work or in deed, do all in the name of the LORD JESUS, giving thanks through HIM to GOD the Father."

I must quote what Pavel said to me as I heard this remarkable encouraging story first hand. "**Woody, there is** a very special peace that comes to you when men hate you, but only if they hate you because of Christ."

Hearing this moving story, there are three words that are firmly placed in my mind: FAITH, FEAR and TRUST! Here we see a brave, faith-filled Christian who treated fear with total trust! God always stands ready to perform miracles when our lives are based on trust and our faith is confidently rooted in HIM. When we treat **fear** with **trust,** all the terrors of life **must go**! Remember HIS promises! In Hebrews 13:5 we read, "I will NEVER leave you or forsake you. The LORD is my helper, I **will not** be afraid." Also in Psalms 55:22, we read, "Cast your burden upon the LORD, and HE will sustain you; HE will never allow the righteous to be shaken!"

You must stop right now and get your Bible and read the Biblical account of almost the same story word for word in Acts 16:23-34. It is true, **"God's word can still be trusted in times of peace or in times of torture, for it is the same today, yesterday and forever!"** Here is another quite profound verse to read in light of this amazing story. II Timothy 2:7 and 9, "Consider what I say, for the Lord will give you understanding in EVERYTHING." "For which I suffer hardship even to imprisonment as a criminal, but **THE WORD OF GOD IS NOT IMPRISONED."**

This particular story has been written about many times and in many books, but here I am, standing before this mighty man of valor for Jesus! What an honor, what a privilege to be here and hear this story for myself! He is known by many of his countrymen as the Conquering Hero. This is a moment that I will remember forever!

Before the night was over, I heard another amazing story that showed me this man's true character, his resiliency for overcoming persecution and his extraordinary sense of humor. His quiet joy just beamed as he shared this very humorous story. It was in the middle of a very cold winter inside the frozen walls of a Siberian gulag that the story began. The temperatures would fall many times to 30 degrees below zero.

Mikhail shared, "The rats were so cold that they would climb up onto the bunks that the prisoners were crowded upon and would huddle to keep warm themselves. They would cover your legs, arms or stomach. One night after kneeling in prayer, I decided that if Daniel could sleep with a room full of hungry lions, I could learn to sleep with a few rats. I could never roll over, however, for fear of crushing one of these small creatures, so I just learned to sleep motionless on my back. God gave me perfect rest each night, and in the morning I would gently brush 15 to 20 rats off me before I would get up. They never did hurt me and I even think they helped keep me from freezing to death."

I just looked at my watch and it is 3 a.m. and I am dead tired. Tomorrow is God's day again. Right now I have to stop and boil some water so that I will have water to brush my teeth with and water to drink in the morning.

Thank you, Jesus!!! My wonderful wife packed me a jar of instant coffee.

DAY 6

Wednesday, August 23, 2000

"And HE called the twelve together, and gave them power and authority over all the demons, and to heal diseases. And HE sent them out to proclaim the kingdom of God, and to perform many healings. And HE said to them, "Take nothing for your journey, not even bread or your extra tunic. And whatever house you enter, stay there, and take your leave from there. And if they do not receive you, when you depart from that city, shake the dust from your feet. And departing from there, they began going about among the villages, preaching the gospel, and healing everywhere." Luke 9:1-6

*"And HE was saying unto them, "The harvest is plentiful, but the laborers are few: therefore beseech the Lord of the harvest to send out laborers into HIS fields. Go your ways, behold, I send you out as lambs in the midst of wolves. Carry no purse, no bag, no extra shoes, and do not be distracted along the way. And whatever house you enter, first say, Peace be to this house. And stay in that house, **eating and drinking what they give you**, for the laborer is worthy of his hire."* Luke 10:2-8

After a bountiful breakfast at Pavel's parents' flat, Pavel shared a very interesting story of this past Sunday's baptism. In a small village not far from Kishinev, there were seven elderly new believers that wanted to follow the Lord into believers baptism. These folks in Russia don't do a baptism with just a sprinkling of water — they do the full immersion in a lake. It does not matter how cold or frozen the lake is either. When a new believer comes to Christ, he or she is usually baptized the very next service. Pavel said they picked out a nearby lake, but when they all got there they quickly found out that they were not welcomed in this town. They were told that they would not be allowed shoreline access to the water. This town had a very strict and fundamentalist Russian Orthodox church, now referred to in Moldova as the Romanian Orthodox Church. It seems the Orthodox folks had been waiting for the new believers to show up. There were about 200 people yelling and shouting and cursing at them. The Orthodox church had organized about 36 people to be standing in the water, waist deep, locked arm and arm, and would not give them an entrance into the water.

To make matters worse, they had been drinking vodka all morning so they were pretty well drunk when the church folks arrived. The police were also there, and they told the Christian group if there was anyone hurt or if any fighting occurred, the police were going to hold them responsible for inciting a riot. After waiting for two hours and hoping that the agitators would give up and go home, they still held firm not allowing the baptism to proceed. These new saints and the rest of the believers decided to go to another lake about 10 miles away, but not before they had mud and rocks and cursing thrown at them. The three Orthodox priests who were responsible for most of the disorder and confusion kept telling the angry mob, "We must stop this evil act because we must protect the heritage of our Orthodox beliefs! We must keep the influence of the 'Western Devil' from destroying our land." The Evangelical Christian Baptists left without any provocation, and late that afternoon the seven people finally became baptized believers in the body of Christ.

The first thing this morning, Pavel and I visited the new site for Pavel's father's church, accompanied by one of the associate pastors. I was informed that Mennonites from the U.S. have given $24,000 for the acquisition of the three acres of land we were standing on. Land is very expensive and almost impossible to purchase privately. Again, the LORD moved and a miracle occurred if they can obtain the necessary permits. And that is a big "IF." They will begin the actual construction when they finish clearing the site. Years of refuse and debris and old run-down shacks completely cover the property now. Every piece of usable lumber has been salvaged. The members will build the new church without any capital campaign and very little money will need to be raised. Pavel shared with me that the members will fast and pray for three days, as the saints of old did in I Chronicles 29, before the actual construction begins. All work will be done with donated labor from church members. Most of the materials will be donated or salvaged from other structures. They figure it will take them probably four to five years to actually complete the church. But the Russian-speaking people have learned great patience! These Christian workers are very trusting and obedient to the pastors that have so bravely led them through many years of trials and tribulations. They have learned that the responsibility of caring for and leading belongs to the shepherd, and the responsibility of obedience and following belongs to the sheep.

I asked Pavel why they have not sought support from their very mission-minded brothers from the Southern Baptist churches in the U.S. Pavel said if they take money from them, the people from America will try to tell them how they should run and build their church. Mikhail Khorev says, "I will take my orders from God and God alone!" Again I say, the church denomination that Pavel's father established is more Mennonite than Baptist in its doctrines.

I should add that since 1906, the American Southern Baptist churches have been very active in their mission work here. Their great evangelical movement was strengthened in 1994, when five Southern Baptist missionary couples were sent to live and work among several small villages in this vast but sparsely populated country. Over many difficult years, the Southern Baptist Church has helped establish over 300 small congregations. These brave pioneers for JESUS have made a commitment to the people, and their presence here has been a powerful force for evangelism!

It was now time to gather up some of the Bibles that our church had sent over. Each day we would only take with us what we were going to pass out for that day. Pavel said that over the course of the week, we would have to travel all through this big city of over 800,000 people to gather up all of the Bibles that COR donated for this mission. I was very surprised when Pavel told me that they had decided to keep God's precious Word at four different sites. Yes, even Bibles are stolen and sold on the black market.

Just some of the 6,500 Russian-language Bibles that we had shipped over and were stashed in four different places to protect them from sabotage and from the Russian Mafia black marketeers.

We ate lunch at Pavel's brother's house with his wife and eight children. Ivan and the entire family had been living and working as missionaries in Kazatstan for the past 10 years. But because of the parents' poor health, they have had to return to Kishinev to take care of them. They live in a tiny home with two small bedrooms and one bathroom, but it does have a fairly nice-sized kitchen. The children have no grass to play on because of the terrible drought — so they play in the dirt. Ivan was in the middle of a major project, reconstructing the home. They were building a huge brick fireplace, stove and oven combination right in the middle of the house. This new fireplace will burn both wood and coal and will serve as heat and a cooking facility when the government turns off the gas in the middle of the winter. Many times last year the government turned off the gas with no warning. If that is not bad enough, all year long many families will go without water and electricity for days sometimes because the government may decide to turn the utilities off without any warning. This is why you never see an empty bathtub. If you are lucky enough to have one, you always keep it filled with water; even though it has to be boiled — it is still water. They also have large cistern-type containers around all the downspouts to collect water for the garden. That is, if it does rain.

Pavel said the drought was so bad this past summer that his 66-year-old mother, Vera, had to stay and sleep in their garden for most of two entire months. Because their garden is 25 miles from their flat, she would have to lug all her seeds, plants, water buckets and tools onto public transportation. The trolleys and the busses would take her to within two miles of their tiny plot of government-allocated ground. But then she would have to walk the rest of the way, carrying everything by herself. This strong, determined and patient woman would spend 14 to 16 exhausting hours each day toiling in their garden. The watering had to be done continually. First, the water had to be drawn by hand from 70-foot-deep hand-dug wells. Then she would have to carry three-gallon buckets of water, two at a time, for over 500 yards. With the terrible drought this year, these life-sustaining plants had to have continual water and nourishment. This diligent woman did all this so her family could eat freshly canned vegetables during the winter.

The only time Pavel's father leaves his flat is to go to church or to visit the orphanages that he so passionately supports. The light hurts his eyes, and it is very difficult to get him up and down five flights of stairs. He has to use a crutch to walk. Remember, there are no working elevators in their 50-year-old flat. Several times this summer some of the members of the church volunteered to come watch the garden so Vera could go and worship. You see, this is just the way it is, and it will be years until it is any better. Everyone is in the same boat unless you are part of the Russian Mafia. You are literally dirt poor. The people from

Pavel's mom and dad. Mikhail Khorev, 69, is known as the "Conquering Hero." Vera Khorev, 66, is truly a testimony to an "Enduring Saint."

poor country is so hard! Everyone has his or her own garden that must be constantly tended to. Every garden has to be protected from the thieves that come at night and steal a winter's worth of survival food. I feel guilty for every bite of food I put into my mouth! Why should I be so privileged to eat this food that this wonderful woman has had to literally slave for? Cheri says, after all, I do need to lose 40 pounds.

You must learn something about the Russian people. They might not eat for a month after you leave, but while you are there as a guest they will feed you their last piece of bread! We Americans waste more food in one meal than these folks have to eat in a week.

Keep in mind, the Soviet Union began its "restructuring" *(Perestroika)* in 1987, but this radical change-over actually continued until August 27, 1991. During this time, it is the smaller former Soviet republics that have suffered the most. The people were just not prepared for what happened over a short period of time. They all did their part as diligent workers under Communist rule. But then the Soviet Machine was supposed to give back to the people! All of the factories and all of the jobs were gone. The people just woke up one morning and there were no jobs to go to. The smaller independent countries that had been under the iron rule of the USSR were instantly broke.

Then, in almost the same time frame as the fall of Communism, the Mafia moved in to fill the vacuum that had been created. Every time an honest person gets a good start and begins to make a profit from their hard work, the Mafia shows up to get their part. If you do not pay them what they demand, first they will threaten you. Then if you do not give in to them, they will kill you. Just like that, one day a creative entrepreneur is beginning to prosper and the next day he is dead. Pavel introduced me to two widows whose husbands were Christians and were killed by this roaming brood of vipers. Pavel told me these brave businessmen refused to bow down to the *Nuva-Ruska*. Now, all the families have left to show for their husband's hard work is a helpless, lonely widow and fatherless children. These women have been left to struggle and provide food for their families and try to make a new life without the love and care of their husbands. Pavel said now the merciless Mafia has threatened and extorted these two helpless widows. If they do not do what they are told, the Mafia will kill the children. It is so awful — one can understand why suicide is rampant. The churches are doing what they can and make great sacrifices to see that these brave and innocent victims of crime are taken care of. But the results of these senseless killings are seen all over the faces of blameless women and children.

Look at some of these poverty incomes. Pavel's mom and dad each get about $7 per month pension from the government. A bottle of water costs 50 cents, and a gallon of gas for the few who can afford a car is $5. The Khorevs' utility bills for the month of August are $54 dollars alone! How do people survive? The answer is that most of them don't. Those that do endure have people, like a Pavel, that will wire money each month to them so they can just live from day to day and be allowed to stay in their flats! If you can't pay for the utilities, after several months the government will turn them off. Then if you do not pay, you will be forced to move to a horribly poor government-run institution. Keep in mind that the individual flats do not have separate utility meters. Most of the time an entire floor is affected. If only one family cannot pay their bills, the rest of the people will also have to suffer by having their utilities shut off, too.

Things are bad now, but wait until September 1. This corrupt government has decided, since they need more money from the people, starting September 1, everyone will have to pay for public transportation! Each bus or trolley ride will be about 50 cents. When Pavel's mom and dad go to church on Sunday, they will have to take three different modes of transportation to get to their destination. So, for the two of them just to go to church one time a week will cost up to half of their monthly pension! The question is, do you want to eat or go to church? Pavel said that he is expecting some very serious protest and possible riots on September 1st. I am glad I am leaving on the 29th. My heart breaks for these brave and patient people who have suffered so much. It seems to me that there is little hope for this generation and very little to look forward to for the next one. Possibly in 30 years things can start to improve. But only if something is done about the corruption and the gangster mentality way of life.

After gathering up the Bibles for the day, we were off to a village 30 miles away called Kerkavov. This small village is truly on fire for Jesus. Their pastor came from Pavel's father's church. In the middle 1980s they became bonded brothers while imprisoned together. Five years ago this brave man started this work for the Lord in a city that had a very predominant Russian, now Romanian Orthodox, way of life. The interesting thing about his decision to move there was the government gave them the land. The pastor and all of the people who felt the calling to begin to evangelize this village were all given a piece of ground for a home and a garden. This sounds wonderful, except there were two big problems:

1. This village has a very strict and hostile attitude towards any change in the Romanian Orthodox way of living.
2. There is no water or sewage disposal or any gas. All water has to be drawn and then carried from one of the village's eight hand-dug 70- to 80-foot water wells. Some of the people that I saw had to carry two three-gallon buckets up to half a mile. (I think I will turn off the water while I am brushing my teeth once I get home!)

Pastor Andre and about 20 families began construction on the church building five years ago, and they are about halfway to completion. They work on the church for a few days then go to another brother's house and work there. Again, all construction is accomplished without any fundraising efforts and all by volunteer labor. True love and dedication flowed from everyone we met.

I had to use the outdoor privy, and I must tell you, I am not ready for this way of life. Pavel made a very profound statement to me after I made some wisecracks about the stinky toilets with no running water. I will long remember what he said, **"Woody, to be an effective missionary, one must not ever have strong likes and dislikes!"**

We arrived in time to walk around the village. When we came to the church building under construction, it was no surprise that they wanted us to have dinner with them. According to our verse for today, we could not refuse. So we sat down to a table filled with 20 very hungry robust, strong Christian men. Again when the food was blessed, I felt guilty. Why should I eat? I did not do any work for my food. These dedicated and faithful Christian men deserved this food. They work very hard each day from daylight until dark, 14 to 15 hours per day. The meal was very interesting, although the only thing that I recognized was some kind of pasta. I had to quote our verse several times while I was **trying** to eat what was set before me.

I sat there thinking about this wonderful group of committed men. I said to myself, "Some day soon, this wonderful temple will be completed. What these men have accomplished here is truly astonishing." Before the wives of some of the men had cleared the dishes off the long, crudely constructed tables, the pastor, who works side by side with the men, began to sing. He got out his guitar that only had five strings; then, just as though it had been rehearsed for hours, the most unbelievable sounds echoed through the half-completed sanctuary. The harmony and the beauty of an all-

The makeshift toilet where Pavel made the comment, "Woody, to be an effective missionary worker, one must never have strong likes and dislikes."

Enjoying our meal with the hungry volunteers of Pastor Andre's new church.

male a cappella choir resounded with what sounded like symphonic perfection. They sang for about 30 minutes while many of the other people began to fill the worship center.

The service began at 8 and ended at about 10 p.m. The reason they begin so late was to give the men time to shower. The workers built a quite ingenious makeshift shower rig right outside that church construction site. Again, with their heads colorfully covered, the women came in and all sat on one side, the men on the other, and the children sat down front. They sang songs that were unfamiliar to me, so I just stood and smiled a lot. Then the associate pastor introduced me and, of course, everyone knew Pavel. I spoke about 20 minutes and told them about COR and our involvement with the Russian-speaking people. Pavel gave the main message. Then once again, the people began to pray as they felt led and continued until the pastor closed the prayer.

Now the fun part began once more. It was my time dedicated to equipping these precious kids. They all came, one by one, and I filled their hearts with the excitement of a Christmas morning. Pavel and I presented the pastors with our special presentation Bibles and signed them, "From all the members of COR."

After everyone had gone home, Pavel and I stayed and talked to Pastor Andre. We had a pleasant visit and a very moving prayer together. Andre shared a touching story about the situation with the hostile Romanian Orthodox Church in their village. It seemed their bitter thinking was based on anything and everything that had to do with evangelical Christianity. He told us that almost five years ago, when they began their work there, the local Orthodox priest and a bunch of the confused flock came to the building site to cause as much trouble as they could. They told them that if a "repugnant empty cross" of any kind was going to be visible from the outside of the building, they would destroy the people and burn the church. Pastor Andre said they all stopped their work and began to pray out loud for these stopped their work and began to pray out loud for these lost and confused Orthodox worshippers. The Orthodox people scattered as the Baptists loudly prayed for a great revival, the kind of revival that would shatter this kind of archaic thinking and bring the people to Jesus. Pastor Andre said that he had asked the hostile priest many times, "Why can't we work together and help each other in reaching this village with the Good News of Jesus?"

It was very unfortunate, but soon after this event, the priest was involved in a very serious automobile accident. He will never walk again. The Orthodox Church appointed a new priest, a young man who was somewhat of a rebel to the Orthodox movement. The first thing he did when he moved to the village was to go to the church construction site and introduce himself to Pastor Andre. He said, "Pastor, I have heard many great and unusual things about you. I would like to make a deal with you. If I were to help you to build your church building, would you help me to build a Christ-centered people to fill my 150-year-old church building?" They began working side by side. This sacrificial act has helped to tear down the walls and bring about a lasting revival to this community of 300 people.

These brothers in the Lord continued the relationship until the Orthodox Church leaders found out about this strange harmonious marriage. The young priest was forced to resign his priesthood. Pastor Andre is now helping the young man and his family get back on their feet. The church is working with them to begin a new work for the Lord in the next community. Pavel and I were so moved by this act of Christ-like love, mercy and compassion that we gave Andre $20 to help this new work. This may not seem like much, but $20 is almost two months of pension money from the government.

We arrived back at the apartment building around midnight. After some writing in my journal, it is now about 3 a.m. and I am bushed! But it is so hot and the dogs outside sleep anyway. I turned on the radio, and I was amazed that I found a Christian station broadcasting some very refreshing recognizable music. Some of the Christian songs were even in English. I got my second wind listening to the music as I wrote about the remarkable events of the day in my journal. It was such a refreshing sound to recognize the "Focus on the Family" theme song. The entire broadcast was in Russian so I did not understand a word of what was being said, although I can be soundly assured that the uncompromising truths of God's word coming from the dubbed-in voice of Dr. James Dobson was going forth and that it would produce some much needed help to these people. A stable and happy family life is foreign to most of the people of Moldova.

DAY 7

Friday, August 18, 2000

"For I was hungry, and you gave ME something to eat: I was thirsty, and you gave ME drink: I was a stranger, and you invited ME in: naked, and you clothed ME; I was sick, and you visited ME; I was in prison, and you came to ME. And the King will answer and say to them, "Truly I say to you, to the extent that you did it to one of the least of these brothers of mine, even the least of them, you did it unto ME."
Matthew 25:40

We had breakfast with Pavel's folks. While we were eating, Mikhail began to tell me a story that is so amazing that it would make front-page press in any major newspaper in America. I have been asked not to reveal all of the facts. They are being kept secret for the protection of the people involved. I do have permission to share the main theme of this hidden atrocity. This astonishing story has only recently been discovered. These surprising KGB documents have been kept in top secrecy for over 60 years.

The story begins when Pavel's youngest brother, Benjamin, was finishing his masters' degree in journalism at the University of Moscow. The subject that he chose for his thesis was *History and the Persecution of the Evangelical Church in the 20th Century*. Somehow, when he was given permission to search some of the KGB archives, he discovered that he had been given access to the wrong information. The documents that were before him were marked "Top Secret KGB." When he opened the first file, he discovered that they had never before been opened. I was told that Stalin himself signed those original documents that Benjamin had in his hands. The lost files are the complete stories of a carefully planned and executed plot by Stalin to eliminate all Evangelical Christians and anyone else that Stalin considered to be enemies of the state.

The genocidal massacre lasted for over two years, from about 1937-38. The total number of files that contain the names and the stories of these martyrs is over 200,000. Benjamin got his hands on about 500 of them. He discovered that late in 1936, people were quickly rounded up like cattle, sent off to a holding prison and then at night were executed. Three hundred to 500 people each night were shot in cold blood, their bodies dumped into trench-like columns of mass graves. Most of the families and relatives were never told what happened to the citizens who seemed to have instantly vanished. But they all had a good idea of where their loved ones eventually ended up. Benjamin made as many copies as he could and has in his possession over 500 of the files. Each document contains the real story behind the undeserving arrest and eventual massacre of these martyrs for Christ. No one has heard all of the details behind this remarkable story, and Benjamin cannot reveal all of the facts until his research and work is completed.

When this story is revealed, what will happen to those who are still alive, those who were responsible for this carnage? Will any of these people ever be tried for even one of the 200,000 crimes of undesired beliefs? When this story does come to the public's attention, Ben's life and the safety of his family could be in grave danger.

This brave man needs our prayers and our encouragement to continue his work until all the pieces to this tragic ment to continue his work until all the pieces to this tragic puzzle are in place, and every story of the martyred saints is accurately documented as to why and when and how. Once this work is complete, the files containing the real truths behind the disappearances will be revealed to any of the family members who are still alive.

What can I say? I am determined while in Moscow to meet with Benjamin and hopefully he will permit me to view some of the files. I hope to see many of the original documents signed by Stalin himself. Pavel said that Benjamin will take me to the actual fields where the bodies of these 200,000 people were disgracefully buried and forgotten for over 60 years. The gravesite is an abandoned marching and drill field. For years, many a Russian soldier has marched, unknowingly, over the top of these forgotten martyrs.

After spending so much time with Pavel's father listening to this remarkable tale of terror, we got a late start. We began the day by visiting the ORA (Operation Reach All) Headquarters in Kishinev. A woman named Veronica Martiniuc heads up this wonderful work. Her work here has been a lifeline of both humanitarian and spiritual needs for thousands of people who, were it not for her, would go hungry. This beautiful lady loves the Lord with all her heart, and she is treated with great love and respect at every institution she is in charge of. I cannot believe all that she is able to accomplish out of such a small and inefficient office. She has none of the luxuries of a copy machine, a computer, a fax machine or any other aid that a modern office would contain. I guess her huge heart for distressed people overshadows the desperate need for decent equipment. Some of her responsibilities include a free medical clinic, free dental office, a tiny drug supply place, a warehouse where she stores Bibles and other Christian literature, a small hospital, a small 30-bed retirement center, and next week she

Just outside her office I witnessed something I have never seen before. Several elderly people were rummaging through the trash dumpsters for food. This was the first, but not the last time I would witness such a depressing sight in this poverty-filled town! The facilities at all of ORA services are free and intended for the elderly and the handicapped, but her door is open to anyone who has nowhere else to turn. We agreed that we will make time to visit the retirement center later this evening.

We then visited the mayor of Kishinev, a Godly man named Vassilie Ursu. What a terribly difficult job he has! People have so many needs and he has no resources to help them in any tangible way. I told the mayor that his job is like trying to stomp out a raging forest fire with your bare feet. He gave us a full hour of his valuable time. Pavel's family and the Evangelical Christian Baptist Churches in the area have helped Vassilie many times. I can see how much influence and respect that Pavel Horev has in this city of almost one million. We walked into the State Department Headquarters building, and we went right to the mayor's office. Pavel told Vassilie's secretary that Pavel Horev and a friend from America were here and wanted to see him. Because of Pavel, we were able to go right into his office, leaving a room full of officials waiting to see this important man. After an encouraging visit, we prayed right there in this man's workplace. On our knees we asked God to bless his most difficult work and bring great revival to the country. Can you believe it, just over ten years ago we would have been arrested and sent to a prison camp in Siberia for four years for just saying the name of God in a reverence to a public official! We gave him 100 of the *I Am Loved* pins and a *Jesus* video and plenty of the *4-Spiritual Laws.*

We left his office and headed to the home for the elderly, supported and run by ORA. We picked up Veronica at her office and drove for about an hour to the small village

Here I am proudly displaying God's Holy Word with the mayor of Kishinev, Vassilie Ursu.

of Starseni. The roads were not fit to drive. The building was in a horrible state of disrepair, but I could not believe how clean it was on the inside. There was no smell of a nursing home, and everything was neat and tidy. These beautiful folks were so happy to see us! As we visited with them, there was no pity because they were out in the middle of nowhere and hardly anyone ever comes to visit them. They were just so happy to be there and have a warm bed to sleep in and decent food to eat.

We talked for some time with the director of this facility, Tatyana. She told us that she and her husband, who is a local pastor in the community, had a great calling to try to do something for all of the homeless and elderly folks in their village. She said that they had sincerely prayed that God would send someone who had the finances to back their noble vision. ORA International came to the rescue. They provide all of the monthly support for the building. Some of the staff is paid and some are volunteers. There are so many needs! No, not needs but HAVE-TOS! They have only a small electric cook stove, and the oven for bread is a makeshift job they built out of some old bricks. How can they fix meals for 30 to 40 people three times a day on a small electric cooktop? They have no dishwasher, but what is much worse, they have **no washing machine**!

Pavel and Veronica Martiniuc (director of Operation Reach-All) standing with some ladies at the rescue home for the elderly.

Can you imagine running a facility of this nature without a washing machine? I can't!

We went to every room and passed out all of our goodies. We gave them a *Jesus* video but, of course, they had no TV, let alone a VCR — maybe someday. These happy and contented saints had absolutely nothing, but I tell you what they did have, LOVE and more LOVE. You should have seen the women's faces light up as we put the *I Am Loved* pins on them and gave them each a precious Gospel bracelet!

We had planned to only stay about an hour, but at 8:30 p.m. we were still there. They insisted that we break bread with them. I must say, I have never eaten such a simple dinner that filled my heart and soul with such emotional thoughts of thankfulness, knowing so many had done so much to make this meal possible.

The home was five miles off the main path on a terrible rocky and dusty road. This building was built as a meeting place for Communist party leaders back in the early '60s. The purpose and thinking was to hide themselves away from the rest of the world so that they could privately carry out their schemes and plots to capture the world and destroy the common working man in doing so.

These 30 beautiful people gave us so much more than the few goodies that we gave them. One lady gave us a flower that she had picked because that is all she had. One beautiful 89-year-old lady read us a poem that she had written to Jesus just after moving to the home. Three years ago she accepted Christ as Lord at the age of 86. This poor but rich saint's glasses were tied around her head with a shoestring because both of the stems were broken off. She was so terribly bent over that when I had my picture taken with her I had to bend over, too. Tatyana said, "She NEVER complains. She loves to read the Bible to those who can no longer read for themselves. She also holds a daily Bible study and leads the services when they do not have a pastor." Another lady gave Pavel and me a little potholder she had made out of the yarn from old sweaters. When she presented her hand-made priceless treasure to us, she began to cry as she held the small cross and pointed to her *I Am Loved* pin and her wonderful Gospel bracelet. She told us how much our words of encourage-

Here I am passing out spiritual laws in Russian, cross in pockets and I Am Loved *pins.*

See the joy and peace she displays on her face from knowing she is a "new creature in Christ."

ment meant to her. We asked her to tell us about how she came to the home. We found out that just two years ago she was homeless and had no family and nothing to eat. Then the ORA home took her in and now she is a believer in Jesus! She is so happy to be surrounded all day long by people who love and care for her. Upon hearing her tear-

The lady who had found Christ was so filled with His joy because she was able to read to others. (Notice her glasses tied with a shoestring.)

filled story, both Pavel (who is not emotional) and I began to cry!

Then all of the women wanted to sing for us and, BOY, was I blown away! What voices and what harmony! God amazes me every time I get out of the way and let HIM do the work and allow HIM to take control of my life!

The men gave me a very different picture. For most of them, blank, cold expressions with a smile being very hard to rise from their toil-hardened and wrinkled faces were all that I saw. They had so much they could say but no desire to express it. Several of them did manage to look at the ground, giving me no eye contact whatsoever, and said, *"Spasiba,"* which is "thank you" in Russian. One elderly man did want us to come to his room to see his Bible. Before we left, we made sure this facility had all the Bibles they would need for a long time!

This "Home for Hope" was as clean and free of smells as any I have ever been in, let alone with what they DO NOT have to work with. Tatyana said that one of the reasons they are able to keep the budget down is the fact that everyone there has a job that they are responsible for. Some of them tend the chickens, some gather firewood for the homemade oven, some wash the sheets, some fold them, some help out in the kitchen, some mend the clothes, some mend the socks, but EVERYONE does something.

The most amazing thing we witnessed was a 14-year-old mildly retarded girl. Tatyana said she just showed up one day, standing outside with no coat in the dead of winter. She has no family and no one in the village knows anything about her or where she came from. So, as Christ would do, they made room for her at the home. Tatyana went on to say, while I was crying like a baby, that this beautiful young homeless girl has brought them so much, too. Every one of the precious old Godly saints wants to baby her and take care of her. (I took this priceless picture and I hope it is good.) While the ladies were singing

The ladies are singing songs of praise and worship — their gift to me.

to us, this former homeless bundle of hope and joy had her head on one of the dear ladies' shoulders. Now, if that story does not bring a lump to your throat and tear to your eye — **check your pulse!**

That night, we began our long and tiring drive back to Kishinev. The terrible roads and huge, almost bottomless, potholes never seemed so menacing. For several minutes that seemed like hours, there was total silence. Then Pavel broke down and that was it for me! Pavel said to me in an exasperated, sobbing voice overflowing with emotions, **"Woody, we must do something to help these people"!**

This work that ORA has begun needs our help. I know we cannot meet all of their needs, but what about a dishwasher and a washing machine and a dryer and enough money to buy a cow or a goat for fresh milk, butter and cheese? Read today's verse again and ask yourself, "What can I do?"

DAY 8

Friday, August 25, 2000

"Whatever you do, do your work heartily, as for the Lord rather than for men. Knowing that it is from the Lord you will receive the reward of your inheritance. It is the Lord Jesus whom you serve." Colossians 3:23-24

"Conduct yourselves with wisdom toward the lost and the unsaved, making the most out of every opportunity, let your speech always be with grace, seasoned, as it were with salt, so that you may know how and when to respond to each person." Colossians 4:5-6

Pavel, once again, had to spend the entire morning trying to get his passport renewed. This is a story in itself. From his home in Kansas, he has been trying— via both snail-mail correspondence and extremely expensive phone calls — to accomplish this for an entire year! After the total runaround he was getting, he decided the only way to break through their bureaucracy of crime and pay-offs was to do this in person. So Pavel left two weeks early to be assured of obtaining a legal and complete passport. This is now his third trip to the passport office! Every time he brings these bribe-ridden people what they have asked for, they think of something else. The officials are all waiting for a bribe and a pay-off. The truth of the matter is, if he would just pay them the $200 under the table that they asked for, he could get his passport renewed instantly. Pavel refuses to stoop to that level of corruption!

I asked him what he was going to do if it came down to the day before he was to leave and they still had not issued him a new passport? Pavel looked at me and sternly said, "Woody, you must have faith in God! HE will provide, and I will never pay the blood money they are asking for!" What a man of faith! I have so much to learn from this brave warrior for JESUS!

While I was waiting for Daniel Apostu to pick me up, I got a chance to leisurely enjoy my instant coffee. Daniel is the very kind man who has so generously given me his flat for the week I am in Moldova. Daniel plans to give me a tour of his experimental farming operation. How he got this farm is another miracle from the LORD! As we drove for about an hour along a terribly bumpy and pot-hole riddled road, he told me the entire interesting story. In 1988, Daniel had just graduated from the university with a degree in agriculture and economics. He knew that God had called him to do something special with his education. Daniel had a vision to start an agricultural and vocational training operation where he could work side by side with the poor and uneducated people in his community, teaching them a much-needed trade.

During the last years of Communist rule, Daniel worked in exports for a government-owned operation that was indirectly involved with a very large winery and champagne operation. Daniel was aware of the many opportunities that would be at his disposal if he would accept the position he was offered and move to the winery. But he also knew that when Communism fell, this extremely profitable business was going to be one of the first targeted for a complete take-over by the *Nuva-Ruska*. As a dedicated Christian, he realized he would be put in a position where he would have to deal and work with this merciless group of people. Daniel said the Russian Mafia proclaims, "We MUST and WILL control everything, including the people that work for us!" Daniel knew that he wanted no part of their ruthless tactics!

His predictions were accurate. Soon after the new government of Moldova declared its independence from former Soviet rule, the Mafia gained a death-like stranglehold and took total control of this huge, very profitable industry.

We drove as close as we could get to the actual headquarters of the winery. The 12-foot-high cement and iron-fortified fences that surrounded the center of operations kept us from seeing much. For miles and miles Daniel showed me thousands of acres of healthy, beautiful, finely pruned vines. The area that we were in right now looked like and reminded me of the Napa Valley! This winery is the biggest industry left in Moldova, and the tragedy is that all of the profits are funneled back to only one family. Mircha Snegur is the man in charge of this corrupt company. When Moldova declared its independence from Russia in August 1991, Mircha Snegur, the Communist Party head of Moldova, was elected the first president. Before the next president took control in 1994, former president Snegur eliminated all competition and made sure that his sons and family would be in complete control of everything pertaining to the winery.

The really sad part about this winery is that some of the finest champagnes in all of the former Soviet Union are processed and bottled here. Because of all the power and the people they control, they have been able to successfully go around the government regulations that are required for legal exports. These products are shipped all over the world. Instead of the entire country benefiting from these wines, only one family receives the benefits. Their wealth is vast and their controls are merciless. Daniel said that just a few weeks ago, ten of the workers were shot and killed for protesting their cruel treatment.

Most of the laborers are not even paid with money. They are given a constant supply of cheap wine for their grueling toil. The wines that they are "paid off" with are of such a bad quality that the company does not even try to market them. Alcoholism pervades these villages. Every one of the villages bordering the winery suffers from this poor and corrupt way of living.

Since it is harvest time now, I see many workers stooping over painfully and picking the lush and prosperous fruit. I grieve for these people, knowing that they will not even be paid for their hard work, and for the fact that the wines and champagne from their exhausting toil will be sold illegally overseas. The real catastrophe is that everyone who buys this product is totally ignorant of the pain behind each bottle. It would be very difficult to offer a toast from the champagne produced and bottled at this huge winery right outside of Kishinev, Moldova!

Daniel did not know how many people were now employed there, but he did say that it is the largest industry in Moldova. But because of who runs it and the way it is secretly operated, they pay no taxes to anyone! It makes Daniel very angry to talk about this, let alone to have to witness this terrible waste day after day.

For several years, after restructuring *(Perestroika)*, he was without steady work. Daniel said he felt called to wait patiently for the Lord's vision and HIS proper direction. Daniel shared with me that during this difficult time he repeated many times, "The Lord is in control and I am only responsible to stay above reproach in my job search. I will continue to seek God's perfect will for my life through prayer and fasting. God will soon give me a vision and my purpose will soon be a reality." Then in 1997, he got a *"chance"* (this word should never be part of a believer's vocabulary) to travel to Holland and represent Moldova in a conference for the importation of farm equipment. Daniel states boldly that it was GOD who sent him to this special meeting. At this convention Daniel met a wealthy Christian brother who showed great interest in what was taking place in Moldova. This meeting was much more than an agricultural conference. The LORD opened a huge door with many unexpected opportunities. The two men seemed to really hit it off as a trusting team. It did not take long for this generous and serving man to catch sight of Daniel's vision.

This generous man has given thousands of dollars to help in the restoration of this run-down farm. The two of them agreed to take some of the abundant resources of the area and turn them into much-needed products. The plentiful existing resources and the vast labor force creates a natural environment for this type of operation. The products and crops produced are sold locally. Prayerfully, maybe someday they will have the opportunity to market them nationally and perhaps even export them.

Right now, under Daniel's supervision, seven local men are working and training. They are learning and experimenting with different ways to process and store cheese. Daniel and his people are also planting diverse hybrid vegetables that grow fairly well in this hot and dry land. Next year they plan to grow several new crops that are totally foreign to the local farmers. He also has three young ladies that work at the farm. They do the cooking for the men, and they are also learning proper ways to prepare and store perishable foods.

I asked Daniel how he came to know the Lord. He told me that it was about eight years ago while Pavel was still living in Kishinev. Daniel was asked to attend a weekly Bible study that Pavel held in his home. After he asked JESUS to come into his life, Daniel became a faithful member of this very devoted group of future Christian leaders.

His deeply committed Christian beliefs call him to employ a combination of Christians and non-Christians at his experimental farming operation. In doing this, he not only employs people in the local community, but most importantly, he helps meet their deepest hunger for spiritual food. The food that will never perish! This great man of God has successfully built and continually travels with his own people over **A BRIDGE INTO MISSION**. Daniel holds a daily Bible study for all of the workers and two times a week he hosts the only church services within 20 miles.

I was ecstatic to find out when we finally arrived at his farm that he also had the only computer in the community with e-mail access! I plan to use this marvelous piece of equipment all night! I need to get caught up with sending my daily messages back to the church.

Daniel has completely surrounded his eight-acre farm with a 10-foot high chain-link fence. He has two guards that work around the clock protecting his operation from theft. He says the biggest problem he faces daily is keeping the local people from stealing him blind. His farm has rich crops and plenty of fine vegetables that are ripe for the taking.

The land that he now works was formerly a prosperous Communist dairy farm. In 1987, this dairy farm employed over 150 people. The last few years the dairy farm was in operation the government was broke so the workers were never paid. Some of these people had worked at the dairy farm for years and they continued to work, even though they knew they would probably never be paid. They kept working just to keep their pension of $7 a month. When Daniel first set up his operation, many of the local people just figured that the crops and the vegetables he was growing were theirs. He has tried to explain to them that he is doing his very best to employ as many local people as possible. He pleads with them not to steal the crops! He has said over and over that he had nothing to do with them not being paid by the government. But his pleas for restraint do no good. These poor people only understand that they are hungry and that Daniel has a bountiful supply of fresh and available food just ready for the picking. Many times the fence has been cut during the night. This is why the grounds have to be guarded 24 hours a day. This farming fortress reminds me more of a prison farm than an experimental vegetable farm.

After Daniel fed Pavel and me and all of the workers with a hearty vegetarian lunch, Pavel and I left to visit a Christian trade school about 10 miles from the farm. What a blessing I found! Two very courageous Christian single women, Lobov Bulah and Nina Maslukova, train and educate over 600 people from 18 to 40 years of age. Most of the students are women, and not just ordinary women — but **beautiful women**! Also employed at the school are six people working in administration, seven staff members and 25 teachers. Most of the teachers are Christians that really have a passion to help these beautiful young people. The school was created out of Lubov's dream and desire to teach and train local youth to become trained professionals in a totally Christian environment. The trades that taught are all desperately needed, service-oriented skills. After graduation, usually in one school year, the students are assisted in finding those greatly needed jobs in their local communities. Pavel shared a fact I was surprised to hear. He said if you are properly qualified, there are many service-type jobs available in Moldova. So for those who graduate from this fantastic school, finding a job is fairly easy. Getting paid is probably another story.

The youth selected to attend this wonderful Christ-centered institution fall into three different categories:
1. Those who can pay all of their tuition.
2. Those who can pay some of the tuition and work off the rest after they graduate.
3. Those who have no money at all and come from correctional institutions or local orphanages.

The skills taught are hairdressing, manicuring, dress design, tailoring, computer and secretarial skills, cooking and restaurant training, and accounting. Besides learning

Two brave women of God, Lobov Bulah and Nina Maslukova, who felt the call to build a Christian trade school where 600 young people go to learn about Jesus and learn a trade — proudly displaying their new Bibles.

a sorely needed trade, the students also have the great opportunity for voluntary daily Bible study. Nearly eighty percent of the students take part in the disciplined study of God's Word. Etiquette and proper manners are also taught and practiced. We went from class to class passing out our *I Am Loved* pins and the *Cross in my Pocket*. We saw that every student and all of the staff got a precious prize from America. I had my picture taken in several classrooms with some of these beautiful young ladies. (This mission stuff is tough work, but someone has to do it!) By the way, while I was there, I got a haircut for about 80 cents, and that was with a fifty percent tip! Even though many were involved in final exams, as we entered each of the numerous classrooms, the students jumped to almost a military-type attention to welcome us. I would share a few words about our mission trip and give them a chance to ask questions. Every one of the students gave me a very courteous curtsy and as well as their full attention and a great big smile.

The school's meager funding comes mostly in the form of grants from companies in the United States and a few local firms that believe in their greatly needed work. Some financial support comes from private donations. The tuition assessments are mostly used to pay for salaries and supplies.

After our tour and a fabulous dinner which was prepared by some of the cooking class instructors, we sat down to talk about how the Lord plays a part in all of this. We were amazed at the dedication of these two brave women, not only to their work, but also to the Lord.

You have to remember that in this country women are considered second-class citizens, and most women do not work outside the home. These two ladies are real rebels with a great cause! We discussed ways in which COR might possibly help them and were surprised at their small requests. The first thing that they asked for was a Russian version

Some of the beautiful students at the Christian trade school. This is where I got my hair cut for 80¢.

of the *Jesus* video. It gave me great joy to reach into my witness tool bag and hand them two of these videos right on the spot. They were overjoyed, to say the least. They said that every Christian group from the U.S. that has come to visit tells them that they will send the school a *Jesus* video, but they never follow through. Because of COR's generosity, we were able to hand them two right there! Praise the Lord! My heart was overjoyed when we got on our knees and prayed for the Lord to continue to bless this amazing work. I might add that their library is now filled with many beautiful Bibles. Before we left, I signed two of the special presentation Bibles and gave them to these wonderful women. They cried and hugged us and begged the two of us to come back on Monday when, once again, another new class of very fortunate pupils would be starting a new year of training.

As we traveled back to Daniel's farm, Pavel and I discussed ways that we could help this wonderful institution once we both got back to America. I have never seen such dedication in not only the staff, but also every student. Each privileged person there knew the importance of having a job and learning a much-needed skill. I wish that many of our youth in GOD BLESS AMERICA could witness what I saw at this God-blessed institution.

Once we arrived back at the farm, Daniel, Pavel and I had some hot tea and a nice visit. The computer and I will be very close friends tonight. I have many days of catching up to do. It is now about 8 p.m. I imagine that I will be up all night! Praise the LORD for plenty of wonderful hot tea!

DAY 9

Saturday, August 26, 2000

"For Zion's sake I WILL not keep silent, and for Jerusalem's sake I WILL not keep quiet until Israel's righteousness goes forth like brightness, and her salvation shines like a burning torch and the nations WILL see your righteousness, and your king's glory and you WILL be called by a new name which the mouth of the Lord will give to you."

Isaiah 62:1-2

I did not stop typing until about 7:30 a.m., realizing that I had typed all night long! Today was the day that I had been looking forward to for many months. This opportunity was the chance of a lifetime to visit one of the most unusual churches I have ever heard of. Even though I was exhausted, I prayed that God would provide me with HIS strength and that HIS anointed Holy Spirit power would keep me going. I hurriedly awakened Pavel, only to find out that he was not feeling well. Daniel was already up and graciously offered to take me to visit the Evangelical Jewish Christian Church. We were running late, so by 8 a.m. I had only had time to eat some bread and slug down some instant coffee. Today was to be another first for me. I have never gone to church without a shower, shave and clean clothes. Pavel said I looked like a Holocaust survivor myself!

The church held services in a rented schoolroom that seated about 150 people, and there was not an empty chair anywhere. The service had already begun when we finally arrived, so we just sneaked in and sat on the floor in the back. As the pastor made some of the usual announcements, our presence soon became known. Pastor Grigore Burlacu and associate pastor Victor Prutiyne minister to mostly elderly Jewish people. These poorest of the poor have no relatives or families to care for them. At one time, most of the congregation was made up of Holocaust survivors. Now all but thirteen have passed on. The exciting fact is many of these courageous souls have accepted Jesus as Lord and Savior. What a beautiful miracle! Pastor Grigore told me that the lives and stories these saints have lived to tell could be a best-selling book. The most important story they have to share is not in their past, but what has happened to them since they have accepted Jesus as Y'shua (the Jewish word for Messiah).

After being introduced as an American evangelist, I began with a bold prayer. My petition to the LORD was, **"LORD JESUS, speak through me this very extraor-**

Pastor Grigore Burlalu and his associate pastor, Victor Prutiyne, during prayer preparations for the baptisms.

dinary day to these beautiful, precious people. May my words be Your words, my thoughts be Your thoughts!" After this loud and resounding prayer, I asked everyone to stand and listen carefully as I read God's Holy Word. I believe reading the profound verses, Isaiah 62:1-2, prepared them for what I was about to say. I shared with them that this declaration was written especially for and directly to the Jewish people many years ago as well as all believers today. I proclaimed, "Every person that has asked Jesus to come into their hearts, regardless of being a gentile or a Messianic Jew, has the enormous responsibility to proclaim the redeeming message of faith in Christ. For HE is the only true and living Messiah and we must proclaim this wonderful message to every person that we know."

I then told them what a privilege it was for me just to be there in their presence and to see all of these smiling faces! It was such a joy to be speaking to this very out of the ordinary group. I expressed this joy by saying, "I have been looking forward to this opportunity since I first met your wonderful pastor months ago back in my town of Kansas City. Pastor Grigore has told me of your difficult struggles and I feel I know all about you. Your powerful determination to spread the Good News of Y'shua to your Jewish friends and relatives is a great victory for the Messianic message everywhere. I wish that I could spend a day with each one of you! To hear your entire life's story would be a humbling experience. To be aware of how your lives have been drastically changed since you have become new creatures in Christ would be a magnificent honor!"

Then the announcement was made as I raised my arm to show them the Gospel bracelets!

"Our Sunday School classes in America have made each and every one of you a Gospel bracelet! After the service today, I will personally equip each person here with one of these missionary tools." I also announced that *I Am Loved* pins, small *Crosses in my Pocket* and plenty of large-print

Some of the members of Pastor Grigore Burlacu's Evangelical Jewish Christian Church.

Bibles were part of the individual gifts they were to receive this day. Then I held up some very special Russian language Messianic literature that I had received the month before my trip from the Jews for Jesus International Ministry. This really got them energized!

Several of them immediately started to get up and were already coming at me when I said with a loud voice, "**After the service!**" Their huge, mostly toothless smiles and their sheer sense of excitement to get them **NOW** should have given me a big indication of what pleasurable chaos was in store for me very soon.

The verse from Isaiah 62 stressed that it was each believer's responsibility to spread the Good News to other Jewish people that might be still waiting for the already arrived Messiah. I continued, "Your testimony for JESUS as Y'shua will have a powerful impact on your families and your community. Your age is not a hindrance but a blessing. Because of the wisdom of your years, many will listen and abide by your words. Each of you can help the younger ones understand what Jesus has done for you. Use your years of experience and knowledge to bring glory and honor to HIS KINGDOM!"

They really enjoyed the story of how COR was begun. At every church and at every gathering, the same story was told. Most of the Russian-speaking people that I have met all have the same ideas about how new churches in America begin. They all think that each new church that we want to start has millions of dollars at their disposal. They believe we simply start a church building and the people will just flood the structure to fill the pews.

My talk ended by telling them they had not been forgotten! Many believers in America were aware of their struggles and were praying for them. I told them again that they were a **very, very special group of people,** and this great honor will be remembered all the days of my life. This was by far the most indescribable event of my life! I do not know what the Lord has in store for me tomorrow, but I do know this — in my 28 years of following Christ I have never had such a humbling and blessed privilege! Looking into the eyes of these brave saints will be a lasting experience that I will share for years to come. I promised them that I would share their story many times and in many churches in America.

When I ended my talk and the benediction was given, I got a taste of what the first hour in heaven is surely going to be like. The joy and beauty that awaits my arrival into the pearly gates of HIS GLORY was before me!

The Gold-rush was on! The people came and stood and cried and smiled and laughed and clutched their prizes and then grabbed for more. They reached with extended arms, and their hands were held wide open with all their fingers passionately pumping for more. Those in front would not step aside to let others behind get in the mad line for the goodies. This left Pastor Grigore standing right in the middle of the unruly crowd attempting to organize the excited and enthusiastic mob of elderly folks.

This remarkable event will stay in my mind forever. It makes me think of a nest full of hungry baby birds. I can just see the mother landing at the edge of the nest offering a big fat juicy worm to the helpless little ones, then watching the totally dependent creatures squawk, flap their wings and hold their mouths wide open for a bit of treasured nourishment.

One elderly gentleman started to carry off my Bible. I did go after him and retrieve it. I started to peel off one of the little *Smile, Jesus Loves you* stickers, but you can forget that! They grabbed the whole card of 16 stickers right out of my hand. Then I took an entire handful of the *I Am Loved* pins to pass out one at a time, and that was not to be either! The only thing that I was sure of was that these wonderful old saints only received one Bible and one of the Gospel bracelets. By the way, my private stash of these priceless leather and beaded gems was getting desperately low. Oh, well! I guess we should have made 2,000, like we did everything else.

This is a really good one! On the top of the package of the *I Am Loved* pins is a very nice and colorful cardboard cover stapled to each package of 100 pins. The multi-colored little sign reads, *I Am Loved* in English — they took those, too! Just think, until now I thought the labels were just trash — but no more.

I was very sorry that I did not get a picture of this semi-chaotic madness, but Daniel could not reach the table to get my camera. I wish every reader could have witnessed this one event. I would have to say what I experienced that day was a *"righteous riot."*

I was almost in tears, I was laughing so hard! People were grabbing anything, but thanks be to Jesus, I had prepared for just such an event. Thankfully, I had packed my Santa's sack full to the brim with the priceless, wondrous little treasures from the generous people at COR! After the battling and hand-to-hand warfare and grabbing of anything and everything had died down, I surveyed the damage wrought by these **"righteous rioters"**; no one was trampled to death on the floor and I did not see any signs of blood nor any gold teeth on the ground!

It was almost an hour before everybody left the building in which the chaotic services were held. I decided to wait until all the wild worshipers had left before we proudly presented these two grace-filled, patient pastors with their very own signed splendid presentation Bibles. They were thrilled to receive such a wonderful present. Thanks be unto God for the wonderful people at Precept Ministries that produce these priceless works of God's Words!

Pastor Grigore and his associate pastor asked Daniel and me to stay for some tea. While sipping our refreshing hot drinks, we laughed as we relived the past hours' memorable events.

Then the pastor came to a serious note when he told us

Pastor Grigore Burlalu (right) and his associate pastor, Victor Prutiyne, just after the Righteous Riot, proudly holding their new presentation Bibles.

that there was a lady we had to meet. The past week she had been very ill so she was not able to attend the service today. He said that we must go by her flat so I could meet her. This Godly man said, "Woody, you have got to hear her story of horror and terror, and her fight to stay alive in the death camp at Auschwitz!"

Pastor Grigore said we would visit her on Monday afternoon after we toured a state-run home for the elderly. He shared that this depressing institution was now the home for many of his parishioners. Most of the people at this poorest of all the government-run facilities had been forced into moving there because they were too poor to pay the utilities on their flats. These desperate people were given no choice — pay off or be moved! How can they pay a $30 utility bill when they only receive seven dollars a month? The pastor warned me about the deplorable conditions that we would see.

Pastor Grigore also shared a very moving story of their last church-wide baptism. He gave me some truly amazing pictures of this wonderful event. Seventeen people over the age of 70, after believing in Jesus as the Christ for the very first time, followed the Lord into Believers' Baptism! What a sight — all decked out in their white robes and hats and many carrying their canes right into the water with them! I shared with the pastor Mark 10:13-16, where Jesus said, "The angels in heaven rejoice when one child comes to Christ."

I then said, "Just think of the shouting and singing going on when one of these saints repents from their sins and turns their life over to the Lord." A brand-new life found in the Living Lord at the age of 70 and more! **Praise the HOLY LORD! May His mighty works never cease**.

We got back to the flat so I could at least clean up and make myself presentable. Pavel was feeling much better now, so after lunch we were off to visit the Vice Premier of Economic Development of the country of Moldova, Nicolae

Baptism is a glorious celebration! Seventeen people over the age of 70 were prepared to follow the Lord into believer's baptism.

Bondarchuk. Pavel said that it was important for me to meet him because of all the powerful me he knows. This one influential man could open many doors for further ministry. He could make it possible for many Christian organizations in America to help the poor people of Moldova.

We were delayed three hours because the car broke down along the road. I stayed with the automobile while Pavel went for some parts to fix the antiquated vehicle. Yes, I was a bit uneasy being left there, but I had my journal in which to write and the Lord to watch over me. I was so tired that I fell asleep and was very glad to be awakened by Pavel and Daniel. In a few minutes the car was fixed and we were on our way. This is the reason I always take with me at least two rolls of duct tape to give away when I go on a mission trip to Russia. After you have been there yourself, you will observe that the entire country would be hard-pressed to function without this wonderful discovery. Any visitor to the former Soviet Union will soon learn that DUCT TAPE IN RUSSIA RULES!

We had a superb evening with Nicolae and his wife, Zhanaw. Pavel said that even though this was not a ministry-type meeting, it was very important for this powerful man to know about the opportunities the people from COR could bring Moldova through business and ministry contacts. We had a very productive three-hour meeting at his lovely home and, of course, a meal that, this time, was fit for a king!

Their son, Sasha, has just moved to Kansas City with kind help from Pavel. He will finish his Masters' degree in law at the University of Missouri-Kansas City. I promised the Vice Premier that we would see to it that our family of friends at COR would take good care of him. Right now, he is alone and knows no one. He is staying in a dorm room with 20 other foreign students. I would like to find a caring family that would take him and allow him to stay in their home for a year.

One of the main topics discussed that evening was the possibility of future economic development assistance from the United States. Nicolae stressed the business and investment opportunities widely available in this land rich with people and vast natural resources. Even though every word was true, I told the Vice Premier that before any U.S. company would consider looking at expanding into Moldova, something must be done to break the horrible vicious cycle of corruption and crime led by the *Nuva-Ruska*. I told him that these bandits must be stopped. Their evil grip of terror and black-market racketeering must be eliminated. I shared that I had seen for myself how the cruel gangs of vipers war against the innocent and honest people of his country. He did agree with me and acknowledged that he was well aware of the evil that was holding his people back from trying to improving their businesses and way of life.

The people all have the same way of thinking: "Why

should we try to better ourselves and improve the places we live? If we do make some positive changes in our lifestyles, the government or the *Nuva-Ruska* will only take it from us!

These gangs of terror have destroyed many local businesses! What it boils down to is this: if the people don't agree and then refuse to succumb to the Mafia's demands, many times their businesses are burned and the owners are even killed.

If an individual or a family decides to fix up or makes improvements to their own flats, they are rewarded in a most sadistic way. Many times, if the government discovers that improvements have been made to a particular flat, the people who did these improvements will be forced to move to another rundown flat many times miles away. The government will then allow their own people to move in to the ones that have been improved. What kind of incentive do these people have to make their lives better with this tainted philosophy?

When we left Nicolae's home that night, we left behind a crystal cross, a *Jesus* video and some *I Am Loved* pins. We brought with us a lot of goodwill and some very positive feelings. This night I was truly an Ambassador for Christ! (II Corinthians 5:20)

DAY 10

Sunday, August 27, 2000

"O come, let us sing for joy to the Lord; Let us shout joyfully to the Rock of our salvation. Let us come before His presence with thanksgiving; Let us shout joyfully to Him with psalms. For the LORD is a great God, and a great King above all gods."
Psalms 95:1-3

"Come, let us worship and bow down; Let us kneel; before the Lord our Maker. For HE is our GOD."
Psalms 95:6-7

Our wonderful pastor, Adam Hamilton, preached on this verse on September 4th, 1999. This was the week after nine of us returned from our '99 Moscow mission. Last year, I made careful notes of Adam's sermon on this most important subject of **Worship**. Here are some of my thoughts of what I believe Adam was saying to me over a year ago about the worship that I was experiencing today. Hebrews 13:8 assures us that Jesus Christ is the same yesterday and today and forever.

1. We must be properly equipped and prepared when we approach worship experience.
2. We must give God the total glory and adoration that He deserves if we are to experience true worship. We

must learn to give HIM continual and never-ending praise.

3. We must praise HIM and glorify HIM with our lives as well as our lips.
4. We must remove any barriers between God and ourselves by confessing any sin we might be harboring.
5. When we worship God, we must come with an open heart and mind, expecting God to work in our lives, to change us into becoming more like HIM.
6. Most importantly, when we give our tithes and our offerings, if they are given as a worship experience, **they must be given as unto GOD**. Our tithes and our offerings may go **through** a ministry or **through** a church or **through** a mission work, but everything must be given as though it was going directly to God.

I like the definition of worship that I heard it explained by Chuck Swindoll. He said, "Worship is the human response to a Divine revelation." I am also reminded of this great man of God's statement on how to approach a true worship experience. Chuck Swindoll proclaims, "True worship is not limited to a particular time or a specific place!"

Pavel and I took public transportation to the church at which we were to speak today. When we arrived around 9 a.m., Pastor Evon Nedeoglo was absolutely elated to see us He told us that the LORD had answered his prayers! He knew that we were speaking in area churches and bringing the Good News and greetings from America. He had prayed that we would choose to worship today in this small, but on-fire, church filled with many excited believers.

The providence of our God was at work again! For this Sunday's worship, we were actually planning to go to one of the villages in the area so I could witness the lakeside baptism of 22 new believers, but I had overslept. I was very disappointed that I had caused us to miss this wonderful event. Because of me, we had to change our plans. But little did I know that my mistake was not an accident at all! We were a direct answer to Pastor Evon's prayers. Romans 8:28 was at work again in my life.

Today was Youth Day at this church. The young man who is the youth director, Sergei Chebotarenco, had just returned from a very fruitful, week-long youth camp. At the camp he had led 63 young people through Bible study, witnessing programs, how to share their faith with others, and training in basic discipleship. Many of the youth who attended camp were from local orphanages. Incidentally, many of these abandoned orphans had never even been inside a church building before today. This Christ-centered youth pastor has now begun a ministry reaching out to these forgotten and troubled young people. Trying to survive in the depressing orphanages of Moldova is a constant daily struggle. At the past week's youth camp, many of them had heard Christ's message of hope, love and forgiveness for the very first time. They have joyfully responded to Christ's invitation of repentance and were given a new life and a new beginning in Jesus! Hallelujah!

I took a wonderful group photograph this morning. This picture will show, for all to see, these smiling and exuberant faces and will literally be worth a thousand words. I see faces that I know will now be able to tell a very different story. On the stage before me, I witnessed young people who had just received a new heart, a new mind and a new start! The most significant thing I saw was a chance for a **new life** that can now be filled with the peace that passes all human understanding! I believe, even when they return to the almost prison-type orphanages, these precious youth will be able to experience a new way of looking at life. Even in those terribly depressing living conditions, the words HOPE, PEACE and JOY will now have a very different meaning. These new Christians can now face life knowing that, "SOMEONE DOES CARE! I DO HAVE A REASON

Pastors Pavel and Evon getting the children ready for their prayer of safety for the new school year.

TO LIVE! I HAVE FOUND OUT WHAT TRUE JOY REALLY MEANS!"

I saw for myself this newfound joy exhibited in the gigantic smiles on each of their precious faces. I believe this same picture of joy is eloquently expressed in the Apostle Paul's writings that so wonderfully describe these joy and peace-filled feelings. Let us carefully examine what Paul said by reading his anointed words. Keep these precious new believers prayerfully in mind as we read Romans 5:1-6, "Therefore, having been justified by faith, we have peace with God through our Lord Jesus Christ, through whom also we have obtained our introduction by faith into this grace in which we stand; and we exult in the HOPE of the glory of God. And not only by this, but we also exult in our tribulations; knowing that tribulation brings about perseverance; and perseverance, proven character; and proven character, HOPE; and HOPE does not disappoint; because the love of God has been poured out within our hearts through the Holy Spirit who was given TO US. For while we were yet sinners, Christ died for the ungodly."

These energized brand-new Christians can also express

this wonderful JOY and true HOPE when they read Romans 8:1, "There is now, therefore, NO CONDEMNATION for those who are in CHRIST JESUS!"

I am sure beginning to enjoy sitting up front and preaching at every service we attend. Oops, there goes my big EGO again. Lord, forgive me! This is certainly not the kind of attitude that Adam Hamilton talked about having when we come to experience God in worship. In the Book of John, chapter 3, verse 30, the disciple whom Jesus loved tells us, "He must increase, that I must decrease."

I now finally realize that all Evangelical Christian Baptist churches pretty much follow the same worship patterns: plenty of bold and wonderful singing, women with their heads covered all sitting on one side of the church, men sitting on the other side, and all the children sitting down front. Everyone stands up for prayers and stands again when the Scriptures are read. When the message has been delivered, they stand again for testimonials and prayer requests. This goes on until the last person who feels led to testify has been given an opportunity. Then the pastor closes with the benediction. Sometimes the new members are recognized at the end of the service, and if there are babies to be dedicated to the Lord, it is done at this time. The breaking of bread always follows, which is usually hot tea and a snack for all!

As I reflect all the way back to the very beginning of that first church in Acts 1:47, I find four key fundamentals that this primitive gathering of brave and bold believers experienced at every worship service. I have been mindful of the fact that every one of the Evangelical Christian Baptist churches that I have visited while on this mission trip have also made these four key elements a vital part of their worship services. I believe that the Book of Acts sets careful, structured precedence for us to take note of. The four essential ingredients that should be present and be an active part of every meaningful worship experience are:

1. Teaching and preaching God's Word (these two very key elements are fundamental, and should always be considered as ONE),
2. Fellowship,
3. Breaking of bread,
4. Prayer.

I am firmly convinced the verse for today (Psalms 95:1-3) certainly applies to the worship services that I participated in these past 10 Christ-centered days. It is such a blessing to see people come to a service and experience true worship and praise. Worshiping without regard to time, or events at school, or what is playing at the movie theaters, or what game is on television or being worried about "We have company coming over in an hour. Won't the preacher ever get finished with what he is trying to say?" You see, for these wonderful Christians, time is about all they have, and plenty of it is dedicated to true and Godly worship.

When you go to Moldova, be prepared for two and one-half to three hours of enthusiastic old-fashioned worship!

At each and every worship experience that we attend, I tell the same story of the history of our church just as I have heard our wonderful pastor, Adam Hamilton, tell it many times before.

It seems that every believer we came in contact with had the same conception about churches in America and the way a new work is begun. They think the first thing we do is to spend a million dollars on a new building, then just open the doors and all the people come, and then you have a church.

Pavel and I both felt like it was so encouraging to these Christians to know how our church began. Even though now we have 8,000 to 10,000 people attending services each weekend, the church was begun only 10 years ago with four people: our young pastor, his wife and their two toddlers. We began COR just like they did — total trust and faith in

God; one man's vision with no money, no land, no building, no people — just a very strong calling and an unquenchable thirst to see people's lives change by the power of the risen Christ! As Adam has said a thousand times, "Our goal and our purpose at COR is to see the non-religious and the nominally religious people come for worship, get involved and then become deeply committed Christians."

At every service I got some great laughs when I shared that our first services were held in a funeral home. I always told the people what Adam said many times, "The people who came to our first church were just dying to get in!" The more I told this story, the more convinced I am that God ordained our church by HIS mighty power. HIS hands and the HOLY SPIRIT have guided our every step. HE knew that someday we would share with believers across the world our humble beginnings and we would use this remarkable testimony to be a great encouragement to other people of vision and faith.

At this Sunday worship service, Pavel brought great words of wisdom from Genesis 3:8-19. He entitled this sermon, "Man's First Divorce," and his message was very appropriately titled. Pavel explained, "Because man chose to divorce and separate himself from God, sin, sickness, disease, sorrow and death have been the dreadful results that have plagued our world ever since this terrible sad and dark day." Even though I really did not understand much of what was said, the Holy Spirit's anointing was covering Pavel as he spoke. People were moved with great conviction, and I saw many a tear flowing from the eyes of people who were seeing the results of this first divorce. Sin has engulfed their land, and the decaying bones of what once was are seen everywhere!

As we traveled from church to church, I would get the same question asked over and over, "Woody, why do our nation and our people have to suffer so much?" This haunting question is one that only God is qualified to answer. But

HIS Word is filled with basic answers. Why does so much suffering have to occur? As long as man has been around to occupy this sin-sick planet, he has asked the same fundamental question. The answer is very basic: it is because we chose to divorce ourselves from God, go our own way and allow SIN to REIGN as the supreme ruler.

I have given much thought and prayer to Pavel's sermon. How true it is, even in our prosperous land of plenty. Man has said, "I have a better way, I have need for nothing. Who needs or cares if there is a God? God is not important to me any more. I will divorce myself from any need of God!" Yet our people, for the most part, have no idea of what real suffering and true poverty is. I pray that our patient, just and loving God will not bring HIS judgment and His wrath upon our people and our land. I pray, "Lord Jesus, help us to see the need for a great revival and that it will begin with me and then spread to the rest of the sin-sick world!" Look at the parable of the rich fool that Jesus told us about in Luke 11:16-21.

On this Sunday, we were blessed to witness 63 wonderful young folks coming up and standing on the stage while Pastor Evon and Pavel individually prayed for each of them. Their prayers were for a safe and blessed new school year. The pastor also talked to those children living in the orphanage. He encouraged them to know, beyond all doubt, that each one of them has a wonderful loving Father who cares for them beyond our human comprehension. He gave them words of great comfort, assuring them that now this church was their new home. God's house is a place where they can always find people who love and care for them. What a message! What smiles radiated from these precious ones. Yes, HOPE and TRUE JOY ARE found only in JESUS!

After this moving and encouraging dialogue with the youth, I followed the two pastors, passing out the wonderful gifts from the generous people from the United Methodist Church of the Resurrection.

After all the young folks were well equipped, I gave their youth director a copy of the *Jesus* video, plenty of extra copies of the *4-Spiritual Laws* and 200 additional *I Am Loved* pins. He said he would use these witness tools for future outreach and evangelism campaigns. He said he would send me pictures of his youth making their own Gospel bracelets, and keep me informed of their spiritual growth. Pavel and I also gave all three of these spirit-filled pastors a signed Presentation Bible.

We had lunch at one of the few Christian-owned restaurants. The pastors and the few people who can afford to eat out once in a great while are trying to help the owners keep their business going. The owner had built the restaurant on years of hard work and had put every dime of his earnings back into the business. Then, as usual, the Russian Mafia moved in and threatened to kill him and his family if they did not pay what was demanded. This brave man and his family refused to give in to these gangsters! By God's Divine providence, the entire family was able to obtain emergency visas on grounds of religious persecution. They boarded a plane and flew to America with just the clothes on their backs. Now, from America, they are struggling to keep the restaurant running.

After a wonderful lunch, Pavel and I took the trolley back to the flat. Hallelujah! I was going to get to spend some time getting my journal up-to-date! Pavel was going to the airport to pick up his new bride, Tatyana. By the way, Tatyana was originally from Moldova, but has not been back since she and her family left in 1991. Boy, is she in for a real awakening on how bad things are!

This beautiful woman of GOD lives in Kansas City. She has only known the Lord for less than a year, but has grown in HIS wisdom very rapidly. Her sweet and gentle spirit glows with every smile. All one needs to do is visit with her for a short time to be aware of God's Holy Spirit working in her life. Tatyana has been a wonderful blessing to us at COR with her generous help at interpreting for our Russian Leadership Institutes.

I was busy writing in my journal until 8 p.m., when Pavel phoned from his mom and dad's flat and told me to come up and enjoy dinner and fellowship with the family. I could not wait to greet Tatyana. It was so wonderful to see her! Here I am, in her former country, greeting her! What a thrill! It was a glorious evening, for she was meeting Pavel's family for the very first time. She was a gigantic hit with Pavel's brother and wife and their eight children when she passed out brand-new shoes for every child! Pavel's brother, Evon, and his wife Lillia are now expecting number nine!

It was very moving for me to be a part of this holy and sacred moment. I gave Vera, Pavel's mom, one of the Waterford Crystal crosses from the Irish Crystal Company. She was overcome with tearful joy at receiving something of such great beauty.

DAY 11

Monday, August 28, 2000

"If a brother or sister is without clothing and in need of daily food, and one of you says to them, "Go in peace, be warmed and be filled"; and yet you do not give them what is necessary for their body; what use is that? Even so faith, if it has no works, is dead." James 2:15-17

Pavel and I spent some time this morning praying over so many people who have so many needs. We were in complete agreement that we take $760 of the mission money from COR and convert it into local currency and distribute as follows:

1. $50 to Pastor Grigore Burlacu's Evangelical Jewish Christian Church, to help buy food for their elderly members.
2. $200 to the Christian trade school for school supplies for the students.
3. $200 to the experimental farming operation to purchase needed equipment for processing cheese.
4. $200 to the ORA home for the elderly that touched our hearts so, to be used at their discretion. Such a small amount to give to an organization with such huge needs.
5. $60 to the man who loaned us his automobile for the entire trip through Moldova.
6. $50 to a single lady we met who was out of work and

had come to us with many pressing needs.

We made a quick visit to all the places listed above. The joy and peace we received in giving the money was an experience of love and true worship in itself. The selfless people were so thankful and so filled with the bliss of knowing that their work and toil had been so greatly rewarded by the generous people from our church's adult Sunday school classes. They were overflowing with the special peace that can only occur in the hearts of those who have the Holy Spirit to constantly remind them that **it is the Lord** that **always gives the true and everlasting rewards.**

Later that day, we visited a terribly depressing state-funded nursing home. Pastor Grigore Burlacu ministers here every Monday afternoon to many of the 200 people who have been placed here by the state. Walking down the cold, dark, drab and lifeless hallways toward a small room where enough light comes in to hold our services, I recognized many of the people. They had attended the services on Saturday at the Evangelical Jewish Christian Church.

I was informed that most of the people here were forced into moving because they were not able to pay for the utilities on their flats. I was even more dismayed to learn that part of the forced-move deal was the people's forfeiture of their $7-a-month pension check. Now, they have no means to work and no money to purchase even the most basic hygienic products.

These poorest of the poor are given only enough food for two very meager meals each day. Their diet consists mostly of bread and a few vegetables. Many times, the food they are given is rotten or spoiled. Survival is learning to live only a day at a time.

This dismal institution has no means of heat during the winter. The only heating available for the individual rooms is the tiny and very dangerous gas cookstoves. Pastor Grigore told us that due to the lack of proper ventilation, the smell inside the institution in the winter is almost un-bearable. These people did not even have chairs to sit on! They sat on stumps of wood!

For most of the day, these empty and emotionless people just stare blankly out of broken windows of forgotten dreams into nothingness. Most of them did not smile or change fa-cial expressions as I placed their *I Am Loved* pins on them. I tried to tell them they are loved by the **One** who truly knows all about their situation, and that **HE does care**! I felt very inadequate and almost guilty for saying such words to people who have been lied to for so long. These precious elderly folks were forced to give up everything that meant home, and move to this place to die! Such deplorable condi-tions would not be tolerated for one day in GOD BLESS AMERICA!

My emotions were raw as I pondered, "Why the huge difference in the people's attitudes at this state-funded home versus the privately funded home we visited only days be-

I had just pinned his I Am Loved *pin on him, and I caught the tear in his eye.*

A woman from the state-run home I visited, proudly dis-playing her I Am Loved *pin.*

fore?" I think the answer is obvious. One group of people had been forced to move to this depressing state-run institution. They will never be given any opportunity for a better way of life. The other, privately funded institution, was filled with people who had been given a job and a responsibility and a chance to be productive citizens. Most importantly, they had been told about finding a new life in Christ! A life that could and would change them completely, offering a brand-new beginning. In one home, the people sang and praised the Lord for all of their bountiful blessings. In the other home, the forgotten residents were left to focus and ponder their now empty lives. All day long they seem to be focused on a life of broken dreams stranded in a wasteland filled with hopelessness.

In a place such as this it has never been more difficult to do the Lord's work. It is very hard for me to deal with these conditions; they are so completely foreign to me. I had to force a smile onto my face, and the words that come out of my mouth were spoken in great love, but they seem to be heard with such emptiness. Yet, I must remember, I was there to care for and minister to God's people. The barrenness I was feeling was not important. The fact that I **was there** and that I **did care** must overshadow my own feelings of helplessness. I must tell myself, "When you are doing the work of the Lord, you must never allow personal feelings or emotions to dictate your course and your callings."

We gathered together about 15 people who expressed a desire to hear our message. We told them the reason we came to this facility was because we wanted them to hear and to know about JESUS. Before we began, they insisted that we share in the very meager meal that they were served. We could not refuse their invitation. After the meal, as I told them the salvation story by slowly going through the different colored beads of our blessed Gospel bracelets, Pavel and Pastor Grigore went from person to person and placed Gospel bracelets on each of them. I shared with them how our church came to be involved with the Russian-speaking people and how I wanted them to know that there are people in America who do genuinely care. After Pavel presented the main message, we prayed with each individual at this humble gathering. I got another glimpse of glory when several of these elderly saints began to sing a very appropriate song, *"Amazing grace, how sweet the sound, that saved a wretch like me!"*

I was dreadfully exhausted from this entire experience, but I knew the HOLY SPIRIT was present and working within me because of HIS strength that I felt. From the depths of my drained emotions, I felt so weighted down! The burden of these folks was so heavy upon me! It was difficult to leave these lonely people. How could words express a farewell? The only thing that I found to communicate was, "By your sweet spirit and the love that each of you has shown me today, I was the one who has been blessed."

Do you remember at the very beginning of this mission trip when I shared the story of a friend named Gregory Parr? This man was a former homeless, inner-city street

A woman holding her precious Cross in My Pocket, *in tears.*

person himself. He found Christ through our church's out-reach program at Westport United Methodist Church. Re-member, I stated that when he shared his testimony at our church, he talked of a new and changed life in CHRIST. Every time he said the word "HOPE," he had us all say "JESUS!" Gregory went on to explain, "When you hear and see HOPE, you must say JESUS!" I can now see the true value of this insightful proclamation in action as I compare the different institutions we visited. One home, filled with people that had HOPE because they were overflowing with so much love. Their HOPE was centered on JESUS! The other home was filled with so much hopelessness because most of the people did not have JESUS and did not care. The thought of what Gregory said resounded in me, and I reflected on the verse in James with which we began our day. Why don't you go back right now and read it again? I think these words will mean a great deal more now than they did just a few minutes ago.

We had two more stops to make on this last very long day in Moldova. We were on our way to visit with the Jew-ish lady from Pastor Grigore's church, about to hear the amazing testimony of her survival in the death camps of Auschwitz. I was so disappointed when we got there that Ardraman Roni was too sick to see us. I gave the pastor one of the crystal crosses to give to her, and we left her with our prayers and love. Pastor Grigore shared with me the entire story of horror and terror that she was forced to en-dure while living through the Holocaust. How she came to his church for the very first time to hear about the love of Jesus is a story within the story.

As the story unfolded, yielding the terrible shocking events, I could not believe what I heard. I wept openly as I listened. Ardraman's story begins in 1943, when this brave Jewish woman had to make to the most horrendous deci-sion of her life. She decided, in order to save the lives of her two small children from the hands of the Nazis, that she had no choice but to give them up. A German neighbor that she thought could be trusted agreed to take them and raise them as her own. The week before the Nazis came to take Ardraman and her husband to the death camps of Auschwitz, she kissed them and said good-bye for what she thought was the very last time. She told the Nazi S.S. soldiers when she was taken that she and her husband did not have any children.

About two years later, the soldiers called all the prisoners out of the barracks to stand on the cold, snow-covered grounds that surrounded their death camp quarters. The soldiers wanted everyone to witness what was about to happen. They called this precious lady out of the crowd and made her come to the very center of the gathering. She saw several men, a so-called priest of some kind, and two small children that she now recognized to be her own precious babes. These horrible, ghastly men asked Ardraman if the two children standing before her belonged to her, and she said, "NO!" They asked her again, and again she denied knowing them. Then while the priest was holding this terrified woman, the two soldiers, laughing and cursing at the same time, drew their military knives and slashed the throats of these two precious, innocent children. She passed out from this horrible, heinous act of senseless terror that she had been forced to witness. She said the last thing that she remembers was one of the children calling her "Mommy."

It is very difficult for me to write this story, let alone think of what this woman has been forced to endure over the years. She had to learn to survive, living with the horrifying memories of her children's lives so carelessly and cruelly tossed away at the hands of such unbelievably heartless men. She has said for many decades, "How could there be a GOD who cares? What kind of God is it who would allow my children to die like this?"

She never knew what happened to her husband, but for many years after she had somehow escaped death herself,

A former Holocaust survivor, Ardraman Roni, who was forced to witness the slaughter of her two children at the hand of ruthless Nazis in the death camps of Auschwitz.

she never told this story to anyone. Then she met Pastor Grigore and saw that this man was different. He seemed to be one of the very few who actually cared about the survival of the Holocaust victims, a man who not only came to visit but cared enough to bring clothes and food. He would listen to their stories of survival and terror for hours on end.

After many visits, the caring pastor asked Ardraman why she would never talk to him about her Holocaust experience. She finally decided that this man was different and that he could be trusted. After all, to these people, trust is something precious and valuable that **HAS to be earned**! The wall had been broken and the veil had been torn! She broke down and shared her story with him. As tears fell, terrible memories of fear engulfed her that day.

This was the first time in almost 50 years she had been able to find the strength and the trust to share this atrocity with anyone.

In 1998, at the age of 92, Ardraman came to church to hear the message of love and HOPE and forgiveness that can only be found by trusting Jesus. She wanted to know, and to be assured, that if she did give her heart to Jesus, someday she would see her children once again, this time in a much more wonderful place than she last remembers. Pastor Grigore has spent many hours with this great woman. One cannot even begin to imagine her life of torment, sorrow and suffering. He has convinced her that the words and promises of Christ are true! Christ would never lie! Ardraman can rest assured that her children **are** with Jesus today, and by trusting in CHRIST, some glorious day very soon she will be with them, too. Oh, what a magnificent day that will be! She will join hands with those two precious little ones in a great celebration! She will be forever in the place where there is no more pain, no more fear and no more tears! A place where beauty is even beyond words we can imagine!

The inspired words of the Apostle Paul ring very loud today with the splendid promise found in Romans 8:18, "For I consider that the sufferings of this present time are not worthy to be compared with the GLORY that is to be revealed to us."

I am so sorry that I did not get to meet this great woman of strength. But I know that someday I will be able to gather with her and those two very special children, and together we can hold hands and glorify and give praises to our Lord FOREVER and EVER!

HE that knows all about horrible sufferings also knows how to give of HIS mercy and to bring about heavenly comfort. Read about this comfort in Hebrews 5:15-16, "For we do not have a high priest who cannot sympathize with our weaknesses, but one who has been tempted in all things as we are, yet without sin. Let us therefore draw near with confidence to the very throne of grace, that we may receive mercy and may find grace to help in time of need."

Even though it was very late, we still had one more visit to make. We were on our way now to visit an elderly, homebound lady who lived with her daughter. The daughter was a single woman, who not only took care of the sick mother, but also had two children to feed and clothe. They had heard that there was an American pastor traveling through their country, praying for people. Somehow she had gotten Pastor Grigore's name and called him to see if he knew who was coming to Kishinev. He assured her that not only was he aware of who was coming, but he promised her that this American lay pastor would pay her a personal visit.

There were no words to describe the living conditions this family endured each and every day. My heart was so heavy from experiencing their ominous poverty. The family had so many needs that I could not even begin to list them.

Every time I think I have seen it all, I have to face another seemingly hopeless situation. When we feel helpless, we must remember that it is never hopeless when we walk with Christ. In the darkest hours of life, we can cry out to Jesus for HIS hands of love and grace to reach out to us and bring us HIS peace and HIS joy. The promise in Philippians 4:19 can bring great security, "And my GOD shall supply all your **needs** according to HIS riches in glory in Christ Jesus!" Here we saw some true needs that must be met! These children did not even have shoes, and their clothes were so torn and tattered that they were not going to be allowed to start school.

The first thing we did when we arrived was to pass out to everyone all the gifts from America. Again, I took time to pray for each person and to make sure that they were given all the individual attention that they needed. As I placed their gifts of love on them, I received such rewards of inner peace. I was so tired and so exhausted from the day's events and yet, now I was filled with the peace that does pass ALL human understanding. In the book of Nehemiah, chapter 8, verse 10, we are offered these great words of encouragement: "Do not be grieved, for the joy of the LORD is your strength."

Pastor Grigore assured the mother that her precious children would be given new shoes and new clothes so they could begin school on time with the rest of the children. He also told them that he and his wife would visit each Monday on the way back from the home for the elderly, and that they would bring food once a week. God is still in the business of answering prayers and performing miracles!

Again I was asked by the single mother, "Woody, why does God punish us so much and why do I have to live and raise my children in such a place?" I told her in a very quiet and humble way that I did not understand why myself, but I did understand that God loves each of us so much and that **HE does care** about their lives. Pastor Grigore told her that he would help her find employment and he would

Two children proudly display-ing their new I Am Loved *pins and Gospel brace-lets. These two children did not have shoes or proper clothes to start school.*

also see to it that all of her family would have a way to get to his church each Saturday for worship. My life was so touched by this tremendous caring man of GOD. The HOLINESS and the GLORY of the RISEN LORD just seemed to shine all about him. I can say without a doubt, that on this day I had truly experienced the presence of angels! When you walk where Pastor Grigore Burlacu walks, you are truly walking on Holy Ground.

The day I arrived in Kishinev, the sight of elderly people digging through the trash to find something edible sickened me horribly. As we left this place tonight, I was even more sickened when I saw children digging through a large dumpster trying to find food. By the end of my stay in this wonderful but terribly poor country, I really thought that I did not have any feelings left. Then I witnessed these poor hungry children trying to survive on decaying, smelly, rotting garbage. When I leave tomorrow for Moscow, completing 17 days of this remarkable mission trip, I wonder what I will feel like. I wonder if it is possible to ever feel normal again? I wonder what our elderly people in America would think if they saw for themselves the deplorable conditions that these folks in Moldova have to learn to endure. Somehow, I must make people in America aware of how blessed our country really is. I must tell everyone that most of the people that we visited today in that home of depression and death are not even buried with dignity. When these elderly homeless people die, they are taken right to the cemetery and then buried in a plastic bag in a grave that is marked only by a number. Just think, you barely survive your life and all you have to show that you even existed is a marker with a number on it. I know that those who die and have Jesus living in their hearts will pass immediately from this life of pain and suffering directly into the arms of our Savior and Lord who has been preparing them a mansion of glory for over two thousand years!

Let us look at what Jesus promised us in John 14:1-3,

"Let not your heart be troubled; believe in God, believe also in ME. In My Father's house there are many mansions, if it were not so, I would have told you; for I go to prepare a place for you. And if I go and prepare a place for you, I will come again, and receive you to myself; that where I am, there you may be also."

I don't think I have ever been so physically, mentally and spiritually exhausted as when I got back to my flat around midnight. I had some hot tea and just sat and meditated on all the brutal but rewarding day's events. The 16 hours of wonderful and blessed ministry to so many hurting souls. I know that what we did will never be forgotten. We were able to touch many people's lives with a ray of HOPE and HIS words of love, but why can't I do more? How can I help these people once this trip is over? "Dearest Jesus, please do not let me forget these people!"

After my tea and a quiet time of meditation, I had to pack for my departure at 8 a.m. for the last leg of my mission trip: Moscow. At 1:30 in the morning I found myself sitting on the edge of my bed motionless, almost numb, and void of any thoughts of my prosperity back in America. I could only think of all of the work that needs to be done here. I pondered on how many people we were not able to see and not able to reach with HIS words of love and HIS message of HOPE. How many people needed to be told about the true HOPE and the love of Jesus, our Savior and our Lord? Every precious one of them! That was why I was sent here to help build a **BRIDGE INTO MISSION**!

I now know just a little of what our Lord must have felt. Many years ago, HE, too, traveled from village to village and town to town. HE saw thousands of people with many needs! HE was moved and HIS soul was terribly grieved because of so many hungry and hurting people. So many people with so little hope! I feel with all of my heart that HE wanted to help everyone and heal all the hurts and pain. Everywhere HE went, there were many great needs! Could HE help everyone? YES, but did HE help everyone? **NO, because HE chose not to!**

Before you draw any misunderstood conclusions on what seems to be a statement from a heretic, please prayerfully and carefully read my thoughts on this delicate matter.

Jesus knew their needs and HE knew their pain. HE so desperately wanted to help everyone HE passed by, **but HE did not**. The question is always, "Why didn't HE do more? Why is there so much pain and suffering?" I believe the answer to this so often asked question can be answered this way. HE knew if that was all HE accomplished while HE was here on this earth; heal, feed, and meet people's physical needs, they would not understand what HIS true spiritual purpose, HIS real mission and ministry, was. YES, HE was — and is — the man of many miracles, great and wonderful miracles. But HE was — and still is — so much more than just a miracle maker. HE helped, healed and fed thousands, but HE came to save **ALL OF US** from our sins, to give us all **eternal HOPE and eternal life!**

We must remember this: there were many that HE did heal and feed, and He made life here on earth so much better by the touch of the Master's Hands, but there were many that HE did not feed and heal.

We cannot help everyone, but we **all can help a few!** I believe that this is the profound truth that drives all mission work. To be effective in reaching the lost for Christ, we must understand clearly the mission of CHRIST!

I reflect on the story of Lazarus' death in the Bible. Mary and Martha were angry with Jesus and even scolded HIM for not being there for their dying brother. After all, Lazarus was one of HIS dearest friends. How could the Messiah be so cruel and uncaring?

Jesus must have felt such sadness and pain at Mary and Martha's confused thoughts. HIS ministry and HIS purpose was misunderstood!

So what did HE do? **Nothing! Not a thing for six en-**

tire days. HE waited patiently and purposefully. After Mary and Martha rushed to HIM, begging HIM to come **immediately** and heal his dying friend, HE chose not to go; He waited. JESUS knew what HE had to do and what HE had to prove to the local religious hypocrites. He also knew what His followers and all of the people that HE loved so dearly must understand. HE was, and is, the only One who could change people's lives completely and forever. HE was not just a man doing good things; HE was GOD in the flesh! Not only did HE have the power and right to raise the dead, but HE also offered them, 2,000 years ago, the same as HE offers us today, eternal life. All we have to do is to believe with all of our hearts that Jesus is who HE claimed to be, our LORD and MESSIAH and SAVIOR!

We can better understand what I am trying to say when we read for ourselves this heart-wrenching story found in John 11:1-35. Maybe now we can begin to understand how HE really felt. We should know now why, "JESUS WEPT!" HE wept because the people were seeing HIM as only a healer and only a mortal man of many miracles.

Yes, HE was able to feed thousands with just HIS words, but we must also see HIM as CHRIST the LORD and SAVIOR for all of mankind.

What great words about some of these amazing miracles are found in John 20:30-31, "Many other signs, therefore, Jesus also performed in the presence of the disciples, which are not written in this book; but these have been written that you **may believe that Jesus is the Christ, the Son of God; and that believing you MAY have life in HIS name.**"

How do you see JESUS? Who is this man that claimed to be GOD? That is the question of all questions! You can answer it now by saying, "HE is LORD! HE IS GOD!"

Keep in mind that one day we will **ALL** be asked this life's eternal question. Do you know HIM as LORD and SAVIOR, or do you just see HIM as a man who lived many years ago and went around doing good deeds?

Even though my feelings have been dulled by so many depressing events, I tell myself that there was so much more in Moldova that I could have done. I will not allow these feelings of inadequacy to control my thoughts and cloud my vision to the possibility of future mission trips here! When I start to feel this way, I will stop and say, **"We cannot help everyone, but we all can help a few!"**

I must caution myself now, just as I do others, "There will **always** be a time of mourning, a time of withdrawal and a time of deep reflection when first-time mission people return from beginning their own glorious voyage to cross the **BRIDGE INTO MISSION**."

We find a wonderful promise stated very clearly in Romans 8:1. I will say to myself over and over these magnificent words that bring me HIS great strength and comfort, "There is therefore now **no condemnation** for those who are CHRIST JESUS."

DAY 12

Tuesday, August 29, 2000

"God is opposed to the proud, but gives grace to the humble. Humble yourselves, therefore, under the mighty hand of God, that HE may lift you up at the proper time, casting all your anxiety and cares upon HIM, because HE cares for you. Be of sober spirit being on the alert. Your adversary, the devil, prowls about like a roaring lion, seeking someone whom he may devour. But resist him, stand firm in your faith, knowing that the same experiences of suffering are being accomplished by your brethren who are in the world."

I Peter 5:5-9

I got about three hours of sleep, and was awakened by the alarm at 5:00 a.m. I had my final breakfast with Pavel, his mom and dad, Tatyana and Daniel. The anointed send-off prayer from Pavel's great father especially honored me. I believe Pastor Khorev's prayer for my protection, asking for the Holy Spirit's anointing and blessings for the rest of my trip, could be heard in Moscow! What a humble honor to have this great man of GOD sign my Bible.

Daniel and Pavel took me to the airport, staying with me until I had to pass through the security checkpoints. As I stood in line to get my boarding pass, airport staff hit me up for $46, for extra weight. Since I had already given away probably 100 pounds of COR goodies, I angrily protested the charge. I had even given away one entire suitcase! When traveling in a foreign land, one must always be mindful that you will not win an argument with the local authorities. So you might as well save your high blood pressure medicine for another time.

I guess I made them angry when I told them, "Of all the airlines I have flown, the people of Air Moldova are the only ones that have had a problem with my luggage." They did not believe me when I told them I had nothing to declare. Thinking back, it seems I probably insulted them when I commented that during my stay I had not purchased any souvenirs. Choosing not to believe me, they made me open all my luggage, and proceeded to go through everything with a fine-toothed comb. I hoped to gain their trust by giving the two officials who were very slowly going through all my stuff one of our "I Am Loved" pins.

They questioned me as to the purpose of my visit. When I told them I was there to tell all the people of Kishinev about Jesus, one of the men said, "Look! I have a cross around my neck." I agreed with him that it was indeed a very nice cross, then offered to tell them about our "Gospel bracelets." They seemed genuinely interested, so I went through each colored bead, just as I had done many times before. I was very pleased when they both took bracelets for every member of their families. Now, all of a sudden, I seemed to be their friend! Well, at least they hurried me on through. But I still had to pay the ridiculous $46 fine for being overweight.

The sad part of the situation was that I had already given away all my personal money, so I was forced to use $46 of the church's mission money. This will not leave me much to help the churches in Moscow, if I ever get there!

All my experiences and all my memories of these gracious, giving people will be good memories. The only part of my entire mission trip that has not been pleasant has been all of the hassles at the different airports. But, to be fair, I think there is more stress experienced in one of our own major airports in the U.S. than on Wall Street. The officials and the airport police really want to make you feel welcome and will encourage you to come back! HA! HA!

While I was walking from the terminal building toward the airplane that would HOPEFULLY — "JESUS" — take me on to Moscow, I soon became aware of why they were giving me so much trouble over the weight of my baggage. The airplane that we were about to board was a jet of some kind, but from that fact on ...well, let's just say we will leave the rest to imagination. I don't know how it stayed together but I am sure it had plenty of miracle-working duct tape holding things in place! The seats were old and ripped and my seat was stuck in the lean-back position making it very difficult to write in my journal. There were no closed overhead baggage compartments so everything that you put up there would just "go with the flow and flow with the go!"

I looked around me and there were no emergency exits one could get to. There was luggage and packages just lying in the aisles. This aircraft should be in the Smithsonian Institute!

I want to end the story of my trip to Moldova on a note of humor. I will certainly have a completely different attitude and opinion about OSHA upon my arrival back in the United States.

I am looking very much forward to landing, and I did say "landing" in beautiful Moscow! My heart does so ache for the poor and the almost **hopeless** situation that I will leave here today. I will never forget my stay in Kishinev, the capital of this once rich and prosperous country. (Remember, "HOPE" means you must say "JESUS!")

These wonderful people of Moldova have touched my soul and sparked such a change in my attitude about life and living in GOD BLESS AMERICA! I said something to my wife, Cheri, just after I had come back from my very first mission trip to Moscow in 1997, that I think is appropriate to quote here. This statement is what I call a

"WOODYISM." (In case you are not familiar with a "WOODYISM," let me explain. Over the years I have come up with many short little trite sayings that I often voice in group situations, such as a Bible study or Sunday School class. They are often seen as a bit corny, but I guess that is what makes them good "WOODYISMS." For instance, one of my best ever "WOODYISMS" is: "I would rather make the wrong decision with the right intent than to make no decision at all!" Here is another good one: "Do the best you can with what you got, but do it NOW!")

Now that you understand what a "WOODYISM" is, let me resume with where I was going in the previous statements.

Just after I returned from this mission trip in 1997, I said to Cheri, "The next time I am having a really bad day at work, I am going to stop and say to myself, **My worst day in GOD BLESS AMERICA is better than the people of Russia's best day could ever possibly be!**"

Please pray for this terribly poor and crime-ridden country. Let us stand in agreement that the revival that has begun there will continue to spread throughout the country and that Jesus' love will spread and reach many of their leaders. Let us pray that the people involved in the "Russian Mafia" will release their choking grip of terror that is currently holding these precious people. Let us prayerfully agree that many of the influential people of this evil group might experience forgiveness and a new life found only in trusting Christ as Lord and Savior.

This horrible, vicious cycle of greed and corruption and power for only a few must be stopped before the living conditions can ever improve. I believe with all my heart that this can only occur if the people's heart and lives are turned to One that can give them true and lasting HOPE, JESUS!

I landed without incident at the Vnukava airport in Moscow. When I cleared customs and retrieved my luggage, I told the Lord, "Lord, here I am — where are your people?"

Not seeing a familiar face after waiting for about 45

minutes, I must tell you, I was becoming a little anxious. I told the Lord again, "Lord, here I am, but where is my ride?"

Finally, by the providence of the Lord, the man that I had been sitting next to on the airplane walked up to me and addressed me in English with a heavy German accent. He asked me if I was the man waiting for a ride to the Methodist Seminary in Moscow. My reply was, "YES, thank you JESUS!" It was then that I recognized this man. He is the bishop of the Methodist churches for all of Eurasia. His name is Bishop Ruediger Minor. I had made his acquaintance only briefly in 1997, but once you have met this brilliant, kind and giving man, you would never forget him.

While we were in flight, he was busy on his laptop and I had my nose in my journal trying to get caught up so I would be ready to begin the last leg of this mission journey. Our only conversation was a greeting when I sat down and again when I offered him a mint after our snack.

The Bishop rode with me from one airport in Moscow to another. I had no idea where we were headed but I was so glad just to have arrived safely that I really did not care. While we were traveling about, we had a very frank and positive discussion about COR's involvement with the Methodist movement in Russia. I was finally told that we were headed to pick up two other pastors that were just now returning to Moscow after an extended stay in the U.S. District Superintendent Dmitri Lee and Pastor Valarie Khe had been in Kansas City attending COR's "Leadership Training Institute" but decided to visit several other cities before returning to Moscow.

After we picked them up, we all had a short but pleasant reunion. They were just as exhausted as I, and ready to go home to see their families, so conversation was minimal.

The driver for the Methodist seminary took me to a location by the airport to be greeted by Pastor Lidia Mikailova. I was told that I would be staying with Pastor Lydia and her family while I was in Moscow. This gracious, patient Christ-loving woman had been waiting for all of us for a long time. Lidia drove us to Pastor Valarie Khe's home where we all enjoyed a wonderful Korean meal. I was truly thankful for the wonderful meal that Valarie's wife, Galina, had prepared.

As I sat there I became a bit overwhelmed at the thought of all of the poverty I had just left behind. After the wonderful meal, Pastor Khe gave me a tour of his church. We did not have to go very far because his house was also his church.

The basement had been beautifully fitted for a sanctuary that would seat about one hundred people. The church also had two separate classrooms adequately equipped for Sunday school gatherings. They also had constructed a small kitchen, and, of course, bathroom facilities. I was amazed at how much work had been done voluntarily to turn this cold and damp basement into a place where many people would come to worship Jesus and have great fun and fellowship.

When we arrived at Lidia's flat, I was pleasantly surprised that Lidia's son Nicholi had a computer with email access! Praise the Lord! At first, I told Lidia that I was too tired to type, but after some hot tea and a cookie, I dove into this machine of such great wonders with both feet. I transcribed my journal into email documents until I could barely hold my eyes open. I fell into bed around 3:00 a.m. It is amazing how I could be so tired yet experience so much strength and energy. It is so true: "Do not be grieved, for the Joy of the Lord is my strength!" (Nehemiah 8:10)

Each time I send my daily messages back to the church, I find new ways of expressing the "joy of the Lord." Each word I send seems to me to be rich in expressions of thanksgiving. Being able to represent my church and the LORD JESUS Himself on these — so far glorious — 12 days of worship is not only an honor but also a sincere privilege! Remember, "True worship is not limited to a particular time or a specific place!" So, with that in mind, I have spent the past 12 long and grueling but rewarding days in continuous "glorious worship"!

DAY 13

Wednesday, August 30, 2000

"Make my joy complete by being of the same mind, maintaining the same love, united in spirit, intent on one purpose. Do nothing from selfishness or empty conceit, but with humility of mind, let each of you regard one another as more important than himself; do not merely look out for your own personal interests, but also for the interests of others. Have this attitude in yourselves which was also in Christ Jesus."
Philippians 2:2-5

Today, I traveled with Lidia for about an hour's drive into the heart of this city of over 11 million inhabitants. I had the extreme honor and humble privilege of being the first American layperson to ever be invited to attend the Annual Pastors Conference being held at the Methodist Seminary in downtown Moscow. To be present at the conference is a great thrill, but if I am asked to address this wonderful group of Christians that will certainly be a huge bonus!

I was gloriously reunited with so many of my wonderful brothers and sisters in Jesus! I greeted them all with HIS love from each person at the United Methodist Church of the Resurrection! Many were pastors and many were young people who would be starting seminary tomorrow. It gives me great pleasure to say that of the 31 people there, I knew all but three.

The pastor's conference began with an opening prayer by our beloved brother in Christ, District Superintendent Dmitri Lee. Pastor Lee then addressed the eight pastors who had just returned from the "2000 Russian American Leadership Institute" that was held at our blessed church. He asked them to be prepared to share a few words with all those who were present at this conference. He wanted us all to hear what this experience and privilege meant for each of the pastors that attended the institute in Kansas City. He also asked them to share the one concept or idea they brought back with them that they will try to implement into their own churches in order to make worship a more meaningful experience for all.

Dmitri Lee was the first of the eight pastors to express his own thoughts. He began by saying, "Every time I return from a trip to America, I feel the meetings that I am privileged to have with our great mentoring pastor, Adam Hamilton, offers me so many new visions and ideas. I am always overwhelmed with great anticipation of getting them implemented and put in motion as quickly as possible with our churches here." He encouraged all the other pastors to keep focused on their own vision and to keep dreaming bigger dreams. He exalted all present to **"Dream like Pastor Adam and never think that you can't do something!"**

He went on to share that he and Pastor Adam had spent some private quality time talking about how they will continue to work together toward the goal of building strong, enthusiastic and growing churches with the limited financial recourses that are available. He told all in attendance, "Some of you younger pastors need to understand, COR began just like we did: no money, no land, no building and no people ... but a great deal of vision and courage!"

Dmitri expressed his desire for the Moscow district of the Russian United Methodist Church (RUMC) to stay focused on membership growth. There are currently 24 churches in the Moscow district, but the vast majority have much fewer than a hundred members each. Dmitri Lee took a bold step of faith as he encouraged the pastors to catch the vision of his plan that he is calling "The Movement of 100." The goal is to obtain 100 members at all 24 churches by the end of the year 2002.

Then he talked about what he wanted to see happen at the 2002 Institute at COR. His main suggestion was his desire to improve the comprehension level of the programs offered. He stated that he and Pastor Adam would work together to devise a procedure of testing what the participants had heard and hopefully learned while at the Institute; maybe a comprehensive four- to six-page test covering all the major topics that were discussed. This could help the participants take the lectures more seriously, and help create a desirable foundation for further discussions of their own thoughts and what they hear from fellow participants.

Another thing that can be looked at, according to Dmitri, is the intensity of the schedule. Dmitri thinks that if every day of the seminar would have more classes and less free time it will help the participants stay focused on the purpose of the Institute and not be distracted by the excitement of just being in GOD BLESS AMERICA! This statement was met with some chuckles and a bit of discussion that I did not understand. When I asked my interpreter, Svetlana Alekseeva, what they all said, she just laughed and replied, "Just Russian talk." Although I must confess I really did not need an interpreter to understand the gist of what they were saying.

I was so encouraged to hear this bold and brave warrior for Jesus direct some pretty strong words of criticism toward some of the younger Christians. Pastor Dmitri Lee said, "You new pastors and those who will begin seminary tomorrow need to be aware of all of the advantages that each of you have that we did not have just five years ago. There is no excuse for you not being involved and busy working in your communities. Inviting people to come and worship and seeing them receive Christ as Lord and Savior is not an option! You have all been equipped with much Bible training, you all have adequate finances available and you all have the proper support here at the seminary! So, don't sit back and wait for the people to come to you! YOU MUST go to the people and make them want to come to your church by showing the Love of Jesus that lives within each of you!"

District Superintendent Lee shared with all present the hopes for a future yearly evangelism conference that would be held in Moscow. He said that he would ask Pastor Adam to lead this first conference, possibly as early as 2001. The idea would be to invite pastors of all faiths and chief lay leaders from the Moscow district and many surrounding villages to take part in this great evangelistic endeavor. He extolled the virtues of our responsibility and our commandment to be busy doing the LORD'S work to help fulfill "The Great Commission."

Finally he offered his sincere condolences to two wonderful ladies, Lidia and Valentina. He gave them his assurance that they would be first on the list to attend the "2002 Russian American Leadership Institute" at COR. These two pastors were chosen to come to our institute this year but they both were denied visas for reasons that made no sense at all to us. He also asked us all to pray for the people at the American Embassy in Moscow who are in charge of issuing visas. Fear of defection, at the present time, makes a visa to America extremely difficult to acquire for anyone who is single. He said, "Pray they would be more sensitive to what was going on and what was actually taking place at these wonderful training institutes held in Kansas City." He was even so bold to suggest that we should pray that the persons in charge of issuing visas would either come to Jesus or be replaced with people that were already courageous Christians.

He then asked Nina Smirenova to be first in sharing her experiences in America, and to tell what she remembered most from the Institute at COR.

Nina told of the great times she had spent with her gracious hosts, Ron and Gloria Duggan. She said that Gloria had kept her "Too busy to get tired." She said the thing she will remember most is the wonderful worship experience the last night at Jim and Rhonda Eynon's house. The singing and the special meal that was centered on the symbols of "breaking of the Seven Seals," taken from chapter 6 of the book of Revelations, was very special. She looked forward to what the Americans from COR were going to teach them next August when we once again would travel to their homeland with another team of lay people that loved Jesus with all their hearts!

Then she went on to share a very touching story. It was an emotional testimonial especially moving to me because I know the power of a changed life in Jesus. She proudly stated, "This 'changed life' occurred at the 1999 youth camp that these loving and devoted lay people from COR held here in Moscow." The miracle she was referring to happened in her own son's life. Eugene had been taught, and boldly proclaimed to all of his friends, that "God only lives in Russia and the Americans could not be trusted!" Nina said after spending three days with the people from COR, Eugene humbly confessed that he had been **all wrong**." It was at youth camp that he gave his heart and trusted his life to the living, loving LORD. Jesus was the one who had the power to change everything that was bad in his life and make it good. He repented of all of his sins and he asked Jesus to come into his life and save him. He now realizes that **God can live anywhere that HE is invited to live!** I was so touched and encouraged by these moving words of simplicity and honesty.

In the past, I have asked myself whether what we say and do on these mission trips really matters once we leave Moscow and return to the U.S. Then I hear a story like this that fills me with HIS power to go on and the encouragement to keep on!

I am reminded of John and Peter's bold testimonial found in Acts 4:19-20, when the religious council in Jerusalem had commanded them to no longer speak or teach in the name of Jesus. "Whether it is right in the sight of God to give heed to you rather than to God you be the judge: for WE CANNOT STOP SPEAKING what we have seen and what we have heard." I also am reminded of the great promise in Isaiah 55:11: "So shall MY word which goes forth from MY mouth; It SHALL not return to ME empty, without accomplishing what I desire, without succeeding in the matter for which I sent it." These two promises alone keep me focused on my job of building a **BRIDGE INTO MISSION**!

Valarie Khe was asked to testify next. He said the thing that he will always remember is how his host family, Don and Sharon Colmenares, had been so kind to these strangers from a foreign land. The principal concept that he learned and will use in his own church was the teachings of Adam Hamilton. The topic he enjoyed the most was becoming more disciplined in your own personal walk with the Lord. He said that he was now properly equipped to face the challenges of helping his own church reach deep into their own souls to become deeply committed disciples of Jesus Christ. Pastor Khe said at next Sunday's worship service he was going to preach with all the boldness that he had seen displayed in Pastor Adam's life.

The next person up was Pastor Vlademere Konevetz. This tall, handsome man shared that his host family, Jeff and Lori Flottman, had made him feel at home in their "wonderful palace." He went on to say that he had a hard time remembering where things were, because the houses in America were so huge! He said, "I felt like a king in a great castle filled with such love and kindness." He especially remembers Pastor Rob Winger's teachings on creating a caring ministry. He boldly proclaimed that he had already read his 50-page manual 12 different times. He said that this important training on "how to become a growing and caring church will be a part of my future ministry efforts." He said he was going to begin immediately to be more disciplined in his personal devotional time. He was amazed that Pastor Adam very seldom slept, and was much impressed with his dedication to his callings. Vlademere expressed a great desire to be more organized with the little time he had to spend with his own family, just like Pastor Adam. He said he never thought it possible for one man to have such a vision. Pastor Konevetz stated that Pastor Adam's vision was contagious to all with whom he came in contact.

Sveta Alekseeva was interpreting for me. She always does a fabulous job, and her interpreting is almost in perfect time with the Russian being spoken. When Vlademere spoke of how contagious Adam's visionary thinking was, I said very loudly, "AH MEAN!" ("Amen" is our English word.) This brought great laughter to the eagerly listening group. Pastor Vlademere ended his talk by calling Adam Hamilton a "great leader and a very brave warrior for Christ's cause!"

Antonina Demeadova began by saying she was amazed at how so many Americans wanted to adopt and love a baby from a foreign land. She confessed that before she went to America and saw with her own eyes, she had always been told that the only reason the rich Americans wanted to adopt Russian babies was to kill them and then sell their organs. I was quite startled by this outlandish comment but continued to listen to this appalling story in expressionless amazement! Then she humbly confessed how terribly wrong this warped and twisted ideology was. God allowed her to witness for herself the real TRUTH. Isn't God wonderful? Look how the LORD was able to straighten out this kind of "stinken-thinken."

God, in all of His providence, chose to put her with host family Paul and Nan Borchardt, who had adopted two babies themselves from Russia. She expressed how much this family loved these adopted children, and how fortunate Alex and Andrea were to have Paul and Nan for parents. She said this devoted family not only loved these babies as their own but, because of these special children, the Lord had given Nan and Paul an extraordinary bonding for the Russian-speaking people. Antonina said because of the wonderful experience she had with this loving and caring family, the most important thing that she learned from this trip was a lesson in love: more tolerance and acceptance for others. She duly noted that when she returned to Moscow, one of the first things that she had done was to share the truth about the Russian/American adopted children.

Antonina was especially moved by the Monday night healing service. She confessed that she had never seen people being touched and anointed like this. She exclaimed with great enthusiasm that her church had already begun to observe this worshipful Christ-like practice. She said that she would never forget all the love and care that she was shown from the people in a far away land called GOD BLESS AMERICA!

Lidia Rodionova said that staying with Ron and Gloria Duggan was "very fun." Gloria kept her busy every minute so she did not have time to miss anything. This quiet and humble pastor was impressed with the spiritual love and the great Bible knowledge that everyone seemed to have at COR. She said that the love she witnessed, studying God's Word through all of our "Disciple Bible Study" classes, was an encouragement for her to begin working on her own church. She was going to tell her church members the importance of knowing and studying God's Holy Word! She felt called, and much more motivated to become a highly effective leader and a more committed Christian in her own church.

Sergei Legastaiev was the seminary student that was chosen to come to the Leadership Institute. He said he especially remembers the lectures about beginning new churches and the evangelism workshop held by Pastor Dave Robertson. He was also keenly interested in how to begin a vibrant youth "Disciple Bible Study" program, such as the one he experienced while he was at COR.

One of the great pleasures I experienced this day was the chance to visit at much length with Ev Erbele. She and her husband Terry are Methodist missionaries for Eurasia, appointed by the United Methodist Board of Global Ministries. Ev and I discussed life in Moscow, and I was able to discern her very deep love and calling to work with these wonderful believers. She shared with me her very Bible-based vision and clear understanding of what the Lord had called her and her husband to do. She told me of several plans to change the structure and rearrange some of the positions currently being held by the people there. She felt confident that some of the people now in leadership were qualified and able to teach others their jobs. They could then work in other areas of ministry. The people that I talked to had great love for these enthusiastic Americans who have dedicated their lives to help the struggling churches in Moscow. I did not get to spend any time with her husband, Terry, as he was in meetings most of the day with Bishop Minor.

I left our frank and involved discussions feeling very good about Methodist pastors being influenced by this tremendous woman's faith and her Bible-based teachings. She impressed me as a woman who is not at all afraid of standing up to those in authority. Ev Erbele is definitely a woman with the people's best interest at the center of her heart. She seemed to be much more interested in teaching good, solid Biblical theology than worrying about who wrote the books being used or the denominational thinking the books were based on. I found her somewhat bold and radical attitude quite refreshing.

What a day of worship this has been! One, indeed, that I will never forget! It was a thrill to sit there and hear firsthand all the wonderful and positive comments from so many people. The importance of our church's involvement in the lives and the ministries of these dedicated people resounded loud and clear. We have truly made a difference. We have given every young pastor great HOPE, "JESUS!" Each seminary student has the "Hope" that someday they, too, might be chosen to come to America and experience this life-changing event. The Russian American Leadership Institute is a cherished event to all who have attended! To be able to take part in this experience, held at the United Methodist Church of the Resurrection in Leawood, Kansas, is an honor that every one of these precious Christians dreams and prays for!

Before the conference adjourned, I felt privileged to be asked to say a few words on how the Lord had called me to work with the Russian-speaking people. I gave everyone greetings from all of our church members at COR in some pretty poor and broken Russian. It is so important to try, even if you probably will "blow" what you are trying to say. The fact that you are giving it a shot means so much to them. Then I made a daring statement that caught some of these tired and drowsy pastors off-guard. I said with a bold and thunderous exclamation, **"In 1995, major bridge construction begins in MOSCOW!"** I paused, waited for a moment, and continued, **"Building a bridge, spanning two continents that will eventually join two great partners for the cause of Christ was the goal and the dream of our great engineer, Adam Hamilton!"**

My loud voice got their attention and now they were all wide-awake. I began my talk by sharing that the designer of this great and magnificent "bridge" first came to explore their wonderful land on his first visit in 1995. While he was here, this idea soon became a vision and the exploration had begun. Pastor Adam saw the limitless possibilities. His plans were discussed, and the groundwork for construction was set to begin when the first group of eager workers came to explore and expand the ideas in 1997. I said, "We planned and we prayed and worked on some language skills for almost an entire year. As hard as it was for Adam, we were all in agreement that for our first visit we would do more listening than doing. I went on to say that this was probably the very first time that Adam Hamilton had ever gone anywhere that he was not told what he would be doing or even where we all were going to be staying. We came here in 1997 with open and willing hearts and minds, filled with so many great ideas and expectations.

I shared with much humor that first morning's experience. Boldly, I said, "All eight of us first-time mission-minded Americans, still tired from jet-lag, gathered in this very room that we are in today. When our eyes met for the very first time, we were all wondering what was going on." I continued, "Some of our fears about the Russian people and some of the fears that you all had about us Americans came to life at that first meeting in late August of 1997."

They laughed at my antics when I acted out the way that we all looked and stared at each other and how we all stayed in our own little groups. I especially made light fun of the fact that for the first 13 days that we were in their country, none of us even shared a meal together. I said, "Remember, all the Russians sat on one side of the room and all of the Americans sat on the other! We all did a lot of staring and a lot of talking about how strange this arrangement seemed. For many years, the leaders of our two countries had wrongly told us that we were enemies. But we soon found out how incorrect that thinking was!" The pastors did remember this and they all laughed at how silly both groups had acted. Now we can all witness and testify to the true and abiding trust and bond of love that has been formed by the power of CHRIST'S never-failing, never-ending unconditional love.

After eight days of hard but very fruitful work, our leader Adam Hamilton began to see this mission was much more than we had first ever imagined. It was not just a one-time mission visit. This was a mission to form a partnership, a trusting agreement; a united effort of both sides working together to build and construct that **BRIDGE** that had now begun from both ends of the world.

I continued to express to the group, "I was fortunate to be in the car that morning with Adam when he shared a bit of this marvelous vision for the very first time with our driver, Pastor Valeri Patkevitch." Adam began to discuss with Valeri, "I see a great hunger and desire in your pastors' hearts to serve the Lord. I also see that there is a huge need for your people to have the proper leadership training and discipleship skills." Adam went on to say, "Valeri, all of the pastors that I have met have plenty of knowledge about who God is. But what you desperately need is a direction or a channel in which you can begin to build and help your small Methodist churches grow in size, as well as in strength." Adam then asked a question of Valeri. "What do you think about the possibility that maybe next year a group of, let's say, ten to twelve of your brightest and most aspiring pastors come to America for two weeks and our church could host some kind of leadership and training institute?" Adam said that the purpose of these seminars would be to properly equip and train the pastors to become more effective in doing the actual work of a church. Building a strong denominational bridge that would reach many for the cause of Christ was to be the mission, and the proper training was to be our goal. The **BRIDGE INTO MISSION** was about to begin!

In 1997, the fact was new believers in Christ were leading most every one of these small Methodist churches. Many of them became pastors because there was no one else to do the job. No one was really prepared for this great mission. Remember, our Lord never calls the qualified, but HE always qualifies those who are willing to hear the call!

That great day in August of '97 this "dream bridge" continued to form, many solid concrete piers of ideas were discussed, and the forms for some solid plans were set in place.

By the time the eight of us returned to the United States, we had also caught Adam's vision. Adam's vision was truly from the Lord: a vision of unifying and building a group of strong and bold believers who could and would now be properly trained and equipped. With this new unifying and purposeful goal for all, these untrained pastors would now have the opportunity to be trained and properly equipped to do the work of the Lord. Giving them this desperately needed training, and by the redeeming power of the Holy Spirit leading and directing them, they could now be prepared to change the direction of many and possibly the course of an entire nation.

I told them that in one year's time, our great and bold leader had challenged and prepared our entire church to catch the vision of the "dream bridge"! The ideas, dreams and this audacious vision became a reality when, in 1998, COR invited the first nine pastors to be the pioneers of the first ever Russian American Leadership Training Institute! "What a great success and an unbelievable experience for all parties involved!" I continued. "Your lives were changed, and so were many of ours. No longer would we be looking at each other with eyes of suspicion."

The construction of this "bridge" was now well underway. Both sides had spent many hours of grueling, arduous work to make the "dream bridge" a reality. It was going to be even stronger than we had ever possibly imagined! By the time we arrived in Moscow for our second mission trip in 1999, construction was well in progress. Then I went on to share how great the reception was when we landed in Moscow in 1999 with a new group of eager mission workers. The hugs and tears of joy and happiness in seeing us again were sincere and genuine, something that I will never forget.

I had tears in my eyes and I was pretty choked up when I said, "From the very first 1998 Russian American Leadership Institute, my wife, Cheri, has also been hooked on you Russians. We were able to have Slava Kim and Konstantin Vaganov stay with us in our home for a glorious time of fellowship and bonding of true Christ-like love. Kosta made Cheri promise that she would be a part of the team of workers coming back to Moscow in 1999." She did come and she, too, was met with much love and open arms and beautiful flowers. I expressed my gratitude for this warm and loving reception when I said, "I have never seen my wife cry with such tears of happiness. There were so many familiar smiling and happy faces to greet her. You see, by the time the nine pastors left America in 1998, Cheri now had met and made many new Russian friends. There in the airport was every one of them! What a glorious time for celebration and what a wonderful experience in 'bridge-building' this was! The bridge construction went great during these wonderfully productive days we spent here in 1999. Again, we made many new and lasting friendships. This time, your youth invaded our hearts. Now the 'bridge' had to be enlarged to also include the future leaders of your nation and your churches in our leadership institutes. We did not come to tell you how to run your churches. We came to just give you our love and to express to you how much each one of you has completely changed our lives. By giving ourselves to you, we learned what it means to give unto Christ."

I was so delighted by the witness of their listening approval. I saw several pastors with tears in their eyes as they sniffled and reached for a tissue.

I concluded my talk by saying, "Now, eight of you have just returned from the 2000 Leadership Institute, and I know by your words today what this training and the experience of 'bridge-building' has meant to you and to your ministry. The story does not end here; it has only begun.

Even now, we are preparing the 2001 team to return in August to listen and learn from you once again. We may have taught you much about what it takes to build vibrant and exciting churches, but you have shown us what it is like to give so generously of yourselves. Your love and acceptance of us has changed the way our church will approach mission work from now on. Many lives will be forever changed as we pass each other over this **Bridge Into Mission**!"

Lidia and I took two women pastors home that night, because it was very late. This way they would not have to use public transportation, which would take almost three hours to get to their flats. As we traveled, I listened to the three women singing songs of praise and worship all the way home. I think the Russians must have twenty verses to "How Great Thou Art"!

Finally arriving home, I sat quietly sipping my hot tea and meditating on all of the day's busy events. I had discovered through discussions with Bishop Minor, Terry and Ev Erbele, and District Superintendent Dmitri Lee that these 24 small but dedicated churches have come a long way since Adam's first visit here in 1995.

We must remember that **they look to us for everything**! We are their strength. We are their financial aid. We are their mentors. We are the main source for most of their ideas and visions. Every program and every ministry that they witness at work in our churches in America will be tried and, if at all possible, they will be implemented here in Moscow.

I was very impressed at how well organized this all-day meeting was. They discussed many other plans, and several other opportunities for further ministries were polished and organized, and would soon be put into motion. A far cry from what we first witnessed on our visit in 1997, when, for the very first time, the Methodists from the East met the Methodists from the West.

Let us not forget, these Christians are very excited about their new faith in CHRIST! We must keep this in mind; it is a very new faith! We must also never forget that when the risen Lord left this earth over 2000 years ago, all of the believers then were just as new to their faith as our new Russian brothers and sisters are today. Look at what the Lord had to work with back then: 11 mostly uneducated, spiritually weak and confused men, and a handful of dedicated women. Just as our Lord was very patient to HIS new church leaders, we must also be very patient with these new church leaders. Most of the pastors of these tiny Methodist churches have only been believers for a very short time. Many ideas of ministry and even basic Bible teachings are still new to them. We must be there for them, to help them along their path toward Christian maturity. Being very patient when they do things that may seem foreign — or maybe even inappropriate to us — is a must. We must allow the churches in Russia to be their own entities, and not force them to try to be just like us. As they strive to follow Christ, I feel it will be the Lord Himself that will lead and direct their unifying efforts to work and pray together. Their efforts are already bearing much fruit. They are not only helping grow a dedicated group of strong and committed believers; they are also doing their part to help fulfill the Great Commission.

When they have invested the time necessary to make their own ideas work and see their own visions become reality, we can begin to see them as truly becoming mature and strong believers in Christ!

When I see these committed Christians hard at work for the Lord, I see the second chapter of the Book of Acts in action. Why don't you read this inspiring chapter right now? I believe you will see and hear what I am saying.

Yes, they have come a long way! But, our "bridge work" here is far from being completed. They still need our prayers, our love, our financial support and, most of all, our one-on-

one personal encouragement. What a wonderful privilege to be part of a church that sees no limits to "bridge building"! God has HIS hands on this "bridge," and is directing every visionary step the United Methodist Church of the Resurrection takes.

DAY 14

Thursday, August 31, 2000

"For I am determined to know nothing among you except Jesus Christ, and HIM crucified"

I Corinthians 2:2

"To the weak I became weak, that I might win the weak, I have become all things to all men, that I may by all means save some. And I do all things for the sake of the gospel, that I may become a fellow-partaker of it."

I Corinthians 8:22-23

I met Konstantin Vaganov and Svetlana Alekseeva and the two of them told me of the plans for the day. We were on our way to visit a city called Seirgiev Pasod. While we were driving, they told me that one of the requirements before they completed their seminary training was to spend a day in this city. Konstantin said that knowing how the Russian Orthodox Church came to power, and understanding why these people think the way they do will be very important to further my ministry with the Russian-speaking people.

Kosta (short for Konstantin) said to me, "Woody, if you are to become an effective Protestant pastor in Russia, you must first understand our people and the history behind the Russian Orthodox Church. The Orthodox Church has survived for over four centuries of religion based mostly on traditions. Because most of these archaic customs originated from the habits of their dead priests, these people live in a constant state of bondage."

Kosta began today's history lesson by explaining that in the late 16th century there was a very radical, non-orthodox Roman Catholic priest that lived in this tiny village. His name was Seirgiev Posad. It seemed that he did not see eye to eye with the Roman Catholic pope and ways of ministry. He began his crusade here after a complete and hostile severance from the Roman Catholic Church. Tradition has it that this man was responsible for many great and miraculous healings. In 1634, when there was no water to be found anywhere for miles, the first onion-dome-topped Russian Orthodox church was built on the very site where Posad supposedly made water come up from the dry ground. This very influential pioneer of the Russian Orthodox movement was the man whose teachings and many traditions are still practiced today.

When he died, his body was never buried. It was taken to the front of the altar in this church and placed in a gold coffin where his bones are revered even today. It was hard for me to appreciate the long lines of people who would stand for hours for a chance to be healed and cleansed from all sin. Tradition has it that this extraordinary event is supposed to take place when you bend over and kiss his dead and decayed bones.

As I stood there and watched this spectacle, I felt such empathy for these people. I wanted to say to them, "This man is not our Savior! He is a sinner just like you and me!" In my opinion, this kind of act is total "idol worship." But as Kosta told me, "This is part of understanding the hostility that the Russian Orthodox people have against anyone who does not follow their thousand-year-old religion based upon very strictly held traditions." As Kosta and I agreed, they fail completely to focus on the finished work of Christ and God's final revelation that is revealed to us in HIS

WORD. They will fight to the death anyone that tries to destroy or change their thinking about their old, archaic ways of worship.

I was totally appalled when I saw a father holding his small child over the bones of this dead and decayed sinner, and making the terribly frightened child kiss the bones. This kind of trauma could disturb a child's mind for many years, and possibly do more damage than I care to even consider. It does not matter how good a man he was, he was still a sinner who needs his sins covered and cleansed by the blood of Jesus! As Romans 3:23 tells us, "We are ALL sinners and we have ALL fallen short of the glory of God."

I also witnessed a woman holding a baby up to a very scary and skinny statue or icon of Jesus and making this child kiss the icon's feet. This skeleton-like statue of Jesus was not a pleasant portrayal of my LORD and my Savior! This hideous icon made the Lord look dreadfully scary and I guarantee that I would not want to kiss the thing! This is not the image in my mind of the Christ that I worship daily. I choose to focus on the Christ that told me in John 10:10 "I came that you might have LIFE and have LIFE in all abundance!"

I saw many people chanting and rocking back and forth. They do this for hours, until exhaustion takes over. Many times people pass out. They think, in performing this type of ritualistic worship, that the more pain they experience the more penitence they will have paid to deal with their sins. I wanted so much to tell them that **Jesus had paid the ultimate price for all of our sins** and that all they are accomplishing is only injuring their bones and joints and bodies.

The young priests that study here can become monks who will never marry, or they can choose to enter into a marriage although this is not encouraged. I heard Kosta share much of their history and a few of their traditions. Hearing these stories reminded me of what the Apostle Paul said when he entered the city of Corinth for the very first time. He, too, witnessed the idol worship of the Corinthians. I know what he means when he said "I have become all things to all men so that I might win some."

Before one can "win some" to Christ, one must understand their way of thinking. That is just what the Apostle Paul did. Now this is what we all must do. We must not condemn them; we must show them the better way, the **only way**. Look at the power-filled, compelling words our Lord Himself said in John 14:6, "And Jesus said unto him, **I AM the way the truth and the life; NO one comes to the Father, but through ME!**"

To truly and completely understand what I am trying to say about Christ and His finished work on the cross, please stop and make a worthwhile investment of your time and read what I call God's chapter about love and mercy and true justice, found in the Gospel of John, chapter 8. There are two verses in this chapter that really stand out; John 8:32, "And you shall know the truth, and the truth shall make you free." and John 8:43, "Why do you not understand what I am saying? It is because you cannot hear MY Word!"

After spending most of the day at this educational and eye-opening place, we traveled back to Moscow. I had a very relaxing dinner that night with Kosta and the other pastor of his church, Pastor Ludmilla Garbuzovia. They are co-pastors of the "Singing Church." Last year, Cheri and I spent our time in Moscow assigned to this wonderful church filled with many professional singers and musicians.

When we had completed a wonderful time of singing, fellowship and a delightful meal, these two visionary pastors wanted to share with me some of their own visions for the future. They told me about a great event they had organized and planned for March 2001. They are calling it "The Ecumenical Music Festival of Moscow." Over 50 choirs from several protestant denominations, a Roman Catholic church and several of the Russian Orthodox Churches will perform both Christian and traditional Russian folk music and dance. This event will last for two entire days and nights. Their church alone pulled off this amazing feat of coordination and organization. To bring all these churches together in one location for this kind of event is truly a miracle. Kosta and Ludmilla shared with me, "Woody, the sad part about this experience is that so many people will be singing about Jesus, but so few will really know HIM as Lord! We want to take every opportunity during these two days to not only sing about Jesus — we want to be prepared and properly equipped to tell all of them how Jesus can come into their lives and change them completely!"

They asked for our help and wisdom in one more of their visions. They shared their ideas about organizing many of the existing Methodist churches to start a radio ministry that would bring singing and Bible teaching into over 30 million homes and flats in Moscow and the surrounding cities. The elderly and homebound of this huge city of over 11 million people share the same situation as the elderly people of Moldova. They have no way to even get to a church! They are so lonely and they live without HOPE, "JESUS," for a better tomorrow. For only a few dollars each day, the possibilities are limitless for an entirely new radio ministry. A radio outreach would reach into the homes of millions with the Good News and the wonderful hope found only in JESUS! These two shared with me that the churches in Moscow could be pioneers in this new mission field. No matter how poor these lost and hungry souls are, most all of them own an old battery or electric-powered short-wave radio.

Their vision brought thoughts of Jakob Lowen and his radio ministry over the Far East Broadcasting Network. I remembered that just recently Jakob had to abandon his broadcast into Russia because the ministry could no longer fund the radio outreach into Moscow. I remember writing in my journal, "$35 a day to reach 30 million people for Jesus! What a bargain for your buck!" I can think of all kinds of possibilities in the union of this wonderful vision with the already established work of our dear friend, Jakob Lowen.

Before I left Ludmilla's home that evening, I gave both she and Kosta one of our wonderful crystal crosses. They were speechless with their presents from the generous Americans.

It was very late when I arrived back at Lidia's flat, but I had some hot tea and then fired up the ole' computer and transcribed my journal until well after 2:00 a.m. The JOY OF THE LORD IS MY STRENGTH! I will have to go back to work if I ever expect to be rested again!

DAY 15

Friday, September 1, 2000

"How lonely sits the city that is full of people! She has become a widow who was once great among the nations! She who was a princess among the provinces has become a forced laborer! She weeps bitterly in the night, and her tears are on her cheeks: she has none to comfort her among all her lovers. All her friends have dealt treacherously with her: they have become her enemies. Her adversaries have become her masters; her enemies prosper; for the LORD has caused her grief because of the multitude of her transgressions. Jerusalem has sinned greatly, therefore she has become an unclean thing; all who honored her despise her because they have seen her nakedness: even she herself groans and turns away. She did not consider her future: therefore she has fallen astonishingly; She has no comforter!"

Lamentations 1:1-2, 5, 8-9

"If my people, who are called by MY name shall humble themselves and pray, and seek MY face and turn from their wicked ways, then I will hear from heaven, will forgive their sin, and will heal their land."

II Chronicles 7:14

Once again, Lydia and I battled the horrible traffic for an hour and a half back to the seminary. I think that this is an appropriate time to share some of my thoughts on Russian drivers and things to watch out for when motoring in Moscow. Driving an automobile in Russia is almost sheer terror. Staying alive and keeping the car headed in the right direction while fighting this insane mob is a feat in itself. Let me make several observations about typical driving habits and several situations that I witnessed:

1. There are no "real" lanes on any of the highways or roads. Even on the superhighways in Moscow, everyone just drives where they want. If your lane is full and the lane coming at you **head on** is not, just "live on the edge" and drive in that one! There is no law telling you that you cannot drive in the "wrong way" lane. The warning "heads-up!" takes on an entirely new meaning!

2. In many areas there are no speed limits unless they are posted. However, speed is not that big a problem. Between the huge potholes one must constantly negotiate and the condition of the deteriorating cars themselves, traveling at an excessive rate of speed is almost impossible, as well as completely suicidal.

3. A red stoplight only means **"stop!"** if stopping is convenient for the driver. If you prefer to just slow down a bit, that is perfectly permissible. Or, if you want to live on the edge again, then go for it!

4. One can park anywhere: sidewalks, in the middle of a road or a major highway, it does not really matter. And one can purchase almost anything imaginable from the friendly street side vendors; from eggs to a truckload of cut lumber, it's all right there!

5. Drivers will just stop, "abandon the ship," purchase whatever — and then they are off again. I saw one place where people parked two deep in the middle of a super-highway because there was no room along the shoulder to stop!

6. One can make a u-turn anywhere and at anytime.

7. One can stop anywhere to pick up a person walking or

you can stop anytime to let someone out of the vehicle.

8. Pedestrians can cross the streets or busy highways anywhere they feel like it.

9. Seatbelts for safety? Boy, there is a misunderstood term for the records! If you buckle up, you have insulted the driver. I was also told that if you want to get stopped by the often bribe-hungry police, wearing your seat belt is a good way to get the local authorities' attention. The reasoning is, if you wear your seatbelt then you are trying to hide something! Seem strange? I wish that I were kidding!

10. I have never in my life seen such small cars carry so much! There is no limit to the stuff one can pile in or pile on! Everything seems to be tied to the roof, sticking out of the trunk, poking through the windows or packed inside. One day in Moldova, Pavel Horev and I saw a tiny car that actually had a large old beat-up and stripped-down shell of another car tied to its roof! That was a sight to behold! This kind of reminded me of the old "Keystone Cops" movies from the 1930s. Who was carrying what, and where?

11. If your car breaks down, you fix it wherever it comes to a stop. Do you remember when you were a kid and how much fun it was driving those crazy bumper cars? Driving on the roads or highways and trying to avoid a broken-down or abandoned car, a pedestrian or the occasional cow or pig is not a far cry from that nostalgic experience.

Maneuvering a car on the sidewalks has become a real art to the brave-hearted driver in Russia. It's nothing unusual to see people turn off a busy road and start driving on sidewalks, frantically honking their horns. Many things on the cars do not work, but the horn is a "must-have" for a successful motorist maneuvering through Moscow. People are well aware that there is no such thing as safe walking or pedestrians having the right-of-way in Russia.

After two weeks of this madness, I wonder if I will feel safe driving again? Just think, my wife thinks that I am a terrible driver! I guess on the mission trips before, we really did not notice the insanity of driving in Russia. We were either too busy visiting with others from our group, or we took public transportation everywhere we went.

Remarkably, I only saw a dozen or so wrecks while in Moscow. Fortunately, I did not see anyone seriously injured. When investigating an accident, I wonder how the police officer decides who is at fault. Probably whoever has the most money to "grease the palm" wins.

Meanwhile, it's back to the seminary in Moscow on Friday morning! Today is the beginning of a new school year. A group of 17 seminary students are about to embark on a fresh path and an exciting journey. Their life will be a path of obedience and a journey of serving. Once again, I had the opportunity to renew old acquaintances with many of the eager, first day seminary students. Many of the new students that I encountered today had attended our youth seminar held in August 1999. It was rewarding to see how these spiritually hungry future leaders of the churches of Moscow had responded to the call from God. Following HIM in obedience to further their education was their next step.

The president of the Methodist Seminary in Moscow is a Godly man named Tobias Dietze. He opened this new gathering of excited believers with prayer. Then songs of praise and adoration were offered to the LORD.

Tobias' message to the new students was a lesson on honesty, integrity and being truthful not only to the LORD but also to yourself and your fellow students. His words were stern but encouraging and supportive to the eager ears. He shared the importance of not only following the LORD in your own individual callings and ministries but also helping others fulfill their goals and dreams and visions. He shared that the work would be very difficult and demanding, but the eternal rewards of following Christ and fulfilling a life of service to others would far outweigh the task. His talk reinforced to me the importance of the Apostle Paul's message in Ephesians 4:15, "But speaking the truth in LOVE, we are to grow up in all aspects unto HIM, who is the head of the church, even Christ."

Of the 17 students who had been accepted into this year's first-year seminary class, most had completed a two-year intensive Bible study that is taught by previous graduates. Although this Bible class is not a prerequisite for attending the seminary, it is highly recommended. I recall a wonderful scriptural promise made to all of us in Isaiah 40: 8, "The grass withers, the flower fades, but the WORD of GOD shall stand forever." Remember what Jesus Himself said about HIS words, "Heaven and earth will pass away, but MY WORDS will not pass away." Luke 21: 33

The key to unlocking real truth and the mysteries of life are at our fingertips. All we have to do to know God's will and our purpose in life is to invest the time to know what HE is telling us through HIS written WORD! "Thy Word, I have hidden in my heart that I might not sin against thee!" Psalms 119: 11. This wonderful promise carries over in the beginning thoughts of the Gospel of John. Have you ever meditated on what those foundational words written by the "disciple that Jesus loved" really mean? Let's examine just a few of the transitional truths that form the very foundation of why we can trust God at HIS WORD and in HIS WORD.

"In the beginning was the **Word**, and the **Word** was with God, and the **Word** was God. He was in the beginning with God. All things came into being through HIM; and apart from HIM nothing came into being that has come into being. In HIM was life; and the life was the light of men." John 1: 1-3.

What you believe about the Bible is up to you. Don't take my word for it, though. As a matter of fact, don't take anyone's word for it! Open God's Word and read it for yourself. Each time you pick up the Bible, simply ask "God, what would you want me to learn from your WORD today?" The more I study, the more I am able to get HIS WORD deep into my very being. I am truly convinced that the Bible is divine in origin, rather that merely a book written by good men. I pray that you will explore the timeless truths and discover for yourself the golden gems of life-changing truths that are found in HIS WORD.

One more verse that we should examine before we go on is one of my very favorite thoughts on what the Bible states about itself. In Hebrews 4:12-13, we find these words: "For the WORD of GOD is living and active and sharper than any two-edged sword, and piercing as far as the division of soul and spirit, of both joints and marrow, and able to judge the thoughts and intentions of the heart. There is no creature hidden from HIS sight, but all things are open and laid bare to the eyes of HIM."

After lunch and a time of fellowship at the seminary, Lidia Mikalova and Sergei Nikolaev and I were off for an adventure on the far side of Moscow. What a drive! The traffic was horrible! An hour and a half later we finally reached our destination: the home of Pavel's younger brother, Benjamin Khorev, his wife and five young children.

As we arrived, we were greeted by the beautiful smiles of their five gracious children. The first thing the children were always assigned to do was bring house slippers for guests to wear. In every Russian-speaking country I have ever visited, you always take your shoes off when entering anyone's flat. There is no grass, and very few sidewalks to walk on; only sand, dirt and mud. Since I did not see a vacuum sweeper in all of Russia, the only way to keep the floors halfway clean is to remove your shoes any time you enter living quarters.

The children escorted us into their small living area where we enjoyed some wonderful singing. These precious little ones sang in beautiful three-part harmony with their

Godly mother leading them while she played the old piano. It was a site and a sound to behold.

While enjoying our afternoon tea and snack with the Khorev family, Benjamin shared his amazing findings with us. We were there to hear, firsthand, the untold story of his discovery of secret KGB files and the subsequent evidence of the mass murders ordered by Stalin himself in 1937 and 1938 of over 200,000 people.

Here is the exact story as it was shared with Lidia, Sergei and myself. You'll remember how Pavel's father began telling me some of the terrifying details of this astounding story, recounted in **Day 7**. Benjamin had accidentally been given access to top-secret files while researching his thesis, *The Persecution in the Evangelical Churches of the Twentieth Century,* for his master's degree in journalism at the University of Moscow in 1998. The circumstances and details of this mysterious disappearance have never been made public. The families never knew what actually happened to their loved ones.

We were spellbound and speechless as we listened to Benjamin share some of the horrific and spine-chilling details of the cold-blooded mass executions. Literally thousands of innocent people, whose only crimes were believing in and trusting in God, were executed. Hundreds of people at a time were shot and dumped into mass graves. Christians, simply put, were a threat to Stalin. This sick man believed the radical beliefs of the Christians would eventually disrupt his devious and cruel plan to control the world. The orders were given, and Stalin's savage, cold-blooded henchmen rounded up over 200,000 of enemies of the state. They were taken to a central death camp in the middle of Moscow. Every night for two-and-a-half years, three to five hundred people were executed under the cover of darkness. The long channels of graves that had been dug during daylight hours were filled each night with the dead. After the killing, the bodies were covered with a 20-inch layer of sand,

and the graves were crushed down into the earth with a huge roller-type machine, readying the site for another night of execution.

As we carefully examined many of the secret files, our hearts were heavy with the reality that the pictures we saw were of real people. People that one day had families, a home and a life. Then, because they confessed that they were believers in God, they were secretly rounded up, imprisoned and killed. Of the 500 files that Benjamin had confiscated, he had completed 37 of the stories of who, what, where when, why and how. We held these individual documents with great reverence. Each completed file included two profile pictures of the individual taken on the day of their capture, the false charges brought against each, the resulting death sentence, and finally, the day upon which they would be executed. Lastly, we stared at the signed "death sentence card" in each of the files.

Benjamin asked us to look deep into the eyes and the faces of the accused. He said, "Look at the cold, empty, staring eyes. These men and women knew they were facing certain death in only a matter of days. Can you see clearly that these saints were not afraid of dying?" Benjamin went on and humbly expressed, "Instead of the dirt and the filth on their faces, notice the peace that passes all human understanding that has been stamped deep into these terribly depressing eyes. These faces beg to not be forgotten!"

Two questions were posed:
1. Why have the surviving families stood by quietly for so long and not demanded some answers?
2. Why has no one ever been tried for these heinous crimes of senseless hate?

Benjamin explained that after all the enemies of the state had been eliminated by the savage actions of the execution guards in the compound, the KGB then killed everyone with any knowledge of the atrocity. Over 2,000 of Stalin's own soldiers were murdered and dumped into the same death trenches! He said eliminating everyone who knew anything became a pretty effective way to keep the whole ugly blight on the country's past quiet. Many of the families had a good idea of what had happened. Rather than question or challenge the brutal leaders of that era, they just accepted the disappearance and eventual deaths of their loved ones as life under the death grip of Stalin, the butcher.

When Benjamin finishes his work, and the files of all 553 people have been given proper acknowledgment and attention, he will turn over the complete history of each person to a remaining loved one. If there is no one living, he will give the files to a church in the city where the person lived and was captured. When this occurs, Benjamin and his entire family will be in grave danger. The KGB members that are aware of what has been buried for so long want the facts to stay buried. Please pray for Benjamin and his family's safety. He told us that he has been called to complete this gruesome task, and no matter what happens to him, the stories of these martyrs will not remain a mystery one day longer than necessary. He boldly proclaims, "My work is being led and directed by the LORD and HE will be our protection and our shield and our fortress! My mission will be completed when the LORD tells me to stop or when HE takes me home. My family understands the risks involved with this calling, and they stand with me." We were truly amazed at what we saw. I held a handwritten document signed by Stalin himself. What a privilege to hear the stories of these martyrs, and to sit with such a brave warrior for Jesus!

From Benjamin's flat, we drove to the actual spot where the murderous acts were carried out. We pushed our way through decaying brick, rotting wood and rusted barbed wire fences. The fortifications through which we crawled were a stark reminder of what had occurred here more than 60 years ago. Eight-foot high walls were all that separated the living from the forgotten dead. What a tragedy! What a waste! What a bleak and horrible reminder of past corruption, sustained and perpetrated by leaders of this once-mighty nation! So many lies…so many needless deaths. But with Benjamin's help, they will not be forgotten, but forever remembered! May the survivors finally find peace. May they be assured that their brave loved ones, who died so long ago, have finally been given proper recognition. These brave souls will someday return with CHRIST Himself and will then be known forever as glorious martyrs for our LORD and SAVIOR.

As we walked onto the large field containing the remains of thousands who died here long ago, I was engulfed with a strange sensation. We were walking on holy, sacred ground. Large, untrimmed trees now surrounded the fencerows, and lush green grass was left to grow on its own, marking the long trench graves. As Benjamin talked somberly in Russian to Lidia and Sergei, I stood quietly alone. The alarming hush that surrounded this "killing field" was so peaceful it was almost ghostly. I observed two remarkable things:

1. The impressions in the settled ground where the graves were laid, in rows upon rows, reminded me of the old drive-in movie theater days. Remember all the rows of man-made mounds of dirt? Those mounds made humps and valleys to elevate the fronts of the cars for better viewing of the movie screen. However, there was no entertainment in this place on this day.

2. In the middle of this huge, empty field was a lone apple tree. It probably has been growing there for years. One lonely tree, all bent over, limbs sagging, almost touching the ground with its heavy crop of luscious, sweet unpicked fruit. As I stared at the tree, I thought it must be trying to say something. The story of what happened here, many years ago, seemed to be hidden in the mystery of the lonely apple tree. I think it was trying to say, "I am very sad to be here. Look at how my branches hang and droop at such sorrowful memories. Remem-

ber what separated man from God in the garden? It was a tree. And because man chose to go his own way, death and sin entered into this now imperfect and sin-filled world. I represent that tree. I am the apple tree of the knowledge of good versus evil!"

The fall of man, the ugliness of sin, the total hopelessness of a life without Christ! Jesus shed HIS precious blood for the forgiveness of all of our sins! The **tree** separated man from God in the Garden of Eden and sin and death resulted. It was also a **tree** upon which Jesus was crucified and died. HE died so that we could be brought back into a right relationship with our Heavenly Father! Galatians 3:13: "Christ redeemed us from the curse of the Law, having become a curse for us — for it is written, cursed is EVERY ONE who hangs of a tree!"

Pastor Lidia Mikalova, myself and Benjamin Khorev's oldest son standing in the middle of the "Field of Death."

We gathered together, standing in silence and holding hands. Lidia began to sing, *"Amazing Grace- how sweet the sound, that saved a wretch like me. I once was lost but now I am found, was blind but now I see!"* I don't think I have ever sung this song with such a sensation of being surrounded by the Spirit and the presence of God.

I read the 11th chapter of the book of Hebrews in a loud and thunderous voice. I felt I had the attention of a huge audience of courageous believers listening very attentively to the God-inspired words I read. I believe these words were written for them. The 11th chapter of Hebrews is dedicated to all the saints in the Bible who have gone on to glory. Many bravely paid the ultimate price for their faith.

Before we left this place of tranquil rest for its many martyred saints, we sank to our knees and prayed for the people of this once proud and strong nation. We prayed and stood in agreement that a great and lasting revival would begin! We prayed that this great awakening would begin in the hearts and lives of the people, and quickly spread to their leaders.

"Dear Lord and precious Savior, may these people never again have to worship in secret. God, watch over them. We pray your protective hand will be upon these brave believers of Russia. May they never have to experience such a horrible atrocity as this remarkable story has revealed! Lord Jesus, may the terror of imprisonment and the fear of death that has surrounded the believers of Russia for so many long and torturous years never be forgotten but never again have to be feared! AMEN!"

The apple tree standing in the middle of the field seemed a bit happier! As we were leaving, we helped ourselves to as many of those tempting beauties as we could carry.

We drove back to town in peaceful silence. Only a few quiet hymns were sung as an offering to the Lord for what we had seen and heard this most memorable day. We appropriately ended the day by attending worship services at

Benjamin's church. He, too, belonged to the denomination that his father, Mikhail Khorev, had founded in the 1960s, the "Evangelical Christian Baptist Church." I am glad we came in late and had to sit in the back. It would have been very difficult to speak to a group today. I would have found it almost impossible to share my emotions and my sense of somberness at what we had just experienced.

It was late when we arrived back at Lidia's flat. I did not feel like sending any email messages back to the church. I had some hot tea and wrote in my journal until about midnight. As I lay there in bed, I reflected on the question I had been asked so many times in Moldova, "Woody, why does our country have to suffer so?" Then the remembrances of this day flooded my soul and filled my spirit with a hunger for revival. I thought of how wonderful things are back in GOD BLESS AMERICA! I told myself that our nation must turn back to God and we must again stand up for what is right and stand against what is wrong! God has so blessed our wonderful country. But with HIS blessings, we also carry a great responsibility. To keep our nation STRONG and FREE we must also keep our nation focused on the principles that have made us this way.

May we read again our verse for today found in II Chronicles 7:14? *"If My people who are called by MY name shall humble themselves and pray, and seek MY face and turn from their wicked ways, then I will hear from heaven, will forgive their sin, and will heal their land."*

I also thought of the nation of Israel. It had many times become an extraordinarily prosperous and bountiful nation under God's constant control. Then it became proud and arrogant and boastful. It was doing so well that its people did not need God anymore. They turned their back on God and they turned away from HIS commandments. They even laughed at the idea of serving only one God. Even a patient, loving and just God will not tolerate this kind of "humanistic" thinking forever! God **did bring HIS judgment** on the people of Israel, as I believe HE has also brought HIS judgment on the nation of Russia! May we turn from our wicked ways, humble ourselves and pray and seek the only true and just God. God was at the very center of our forefathers' minds when our great nation was first established. Our nation was built upon religious freedom for all! May we always be, *"One nation, UNDER GOD, with liberty and justice for ALL!"*

DAY 16

Saturday, September 2, 2000

"And the glory which Thou hast given ME I have given to them: that they may be one, just as WE are one."

John 17:22

"And I have made Thy name known to them, and will continue to make it known to them; that the love wherewith Thou didst love ME may be in them, and I in them."

John 17:26

Today we were on a journey of preaching, teaching and sharing the love of Jesus with two Methodist churches in the central Moscow area. Both churches, because of where they are located, hold worship services on Saturday. The public transportation seems to be much more accommodating on this day.

How honored I felt to be asked to bring a message from the Lord today. There are no words with which I can fully convey my JOY and the excitement I feel when I am asked to preach and teach the rich truths from God's WORD. I am always prepared to share the simple and practical lessons about life that I have learned and experienced from studying and actually **living the Bible**. I can honestly say that I have learned to give thanks to the LORD for the many dead-end, dusty roads that I have traveled. The LORD has allowed me the privilege to journey through some pretty rough miles in my 28-year pilgrimage with Christ. Now it is my turn, my calling; and I feel my mandate to share many of these difficult crusades so I can encourage others in their journeys. "Rejoice always; pray without ceasing; in EVERY-THING give thanks for this is God's will for you in Christ Jesus." I Thessalonians 5:16-18. My humble prayer is to see that in everything that I do, all praise, honor and glory will go to HIM. As I said in the very beginning of this journal, I want my life to be a mirror that will constantly reflect God's glory.

We arrived early enough at Valentina's church, The Tree of Life, to pray and just sit quietly. Today was my last full day in Russia until August of 2001. This somber thought brought me both joy and sadness as I sat and meditated on what I had seen, heard and done for the Lord. These past 16 days have changed my life forever. As I pondered the goodness of God, I reflected on how this mission trip was first a dream, and then a vision, and then it became a

"Tree of Life" Methodist Church in Moscow. Pastor and interpreter Sveta Alekseeva translated the message as I shared the meaning of the gospel bracelet.

prayer-filled goal of faith and trust in HIM! These thoughts led me to open my Bible and read Habakkuk 2:3-5, "For the vision is yet for the appointed time; It hastens toward the goal, and it will not fail. Though it tarries, wait for it; for it will certainly come, it will not delay. Behold, as for the proud one, his soul is not right within him; but the **RIGHTEOUS will live by faith!**"

After my brief introduction and the usual greetings, the WORD that I felt the LORD wanted me to bring was found in the Gospel of John, chapter 21, verses 3 through 13. I titled my message **"Should I go back to my old way of life?"** I began by asking a question in an almost deafening voice. **"Where is my best friend, JESUS, when I needed HIM the most?"**

I paused, looking around at the people. For about one minute I said nothing else. The people were a bit shaken by my thunderous beginning but sat quietly waiting for my next words. I stood there with a blank, and empty "have I gone astray?" look on my face. I acted out the feelings of desperation and anxiousness that these confused disciples must have been experiencing. As I read the story in John 21, verse-by-verse, I played the roles and spoke the dialogues of possible conversations the disciples might have had with one another.

I expressed my next series of piercing questions.

"It has been eight long, lonely and frightening days since we have seen HIM. Is it all over for us, now that everyone knows of HIS crucifixion and death?

"Should we leave the upper room and go out into the world to be killed like HE was?

"Should we just stay here and wait for HIS return? How long will we wait?

"What are we all to do? HE told us that HE was going to come again. But WHEN will it be?

"We need some directions! We need a reason and

a purpose to carry out HIS message ... or should we even bother?

"Who will lead us now?

"Are we going to suffer and die like HE did?

"Where is this 'comforter' that HE talked about so much?

"What is this 'comforter,' anyway?"

Once again, after the interpretation, I paused and waited for about a minute. People were staring at me with a bit of wonderment, trying to anticipate my next dialogue. There was total silence! Finally, speaking after what seemed like an eternity, I played the part of BOLD and IMPETUOUS Peter.

"I don't know about you guys, but I AM GOING FISHING!"

I continued my message, using facial expressions and role-playing Peter at the same time.

"I am going back to my old ways of life, my life before this radical Man, Jesus, came and told us to leave everything and follow HIM. For what? Where is HE now when we need HIM the most?

"We all have given up our jobs, our families, our futures, our security and every resemblance of a normal life! What do we have to show for following HIM?

"For three whole years we have dedicated ourselves to HIS mission — FOR WHAT?

"Where is this KINGDOM of GOD that HE talked so much about? If HE really cared about us, HE would not have left us all alone.

"Yes, and whatever this 'comforter' is....will HE send it to us as HE promised?"

Then the others said, "We are tired of waiting, too. We will follow you, Peter!"

As you read this marvelous story you can feel the disciples' intense emotions. Most importantly, though, you will discover that Jesus **did not leave them nor forsake**

them. In the midnight hour, when they needed HIM the most, He came to them, called them HIS little children and told them to put their nets on the RIGHT side of the boat. HE blessed them with the largest catch they had ever seen. That faith-filled morning, 153 large fish overflowed the unbroken net. Not one fish escaped the netting and yet it was not torn! In that unbroken mesh of slender strands of rope was one of each type of fish, representing every species known to man at that time. This scene also represented to the disciples the great call, the commission to go out, into the entire world and preach the WORD to every living tribe and every existing nation.

The disciples had worked hard all night long but had caught nothing. Jesus knew how desperate they were. HE knew how much they needed, once again, HIS direction and HIS gentle touch. So HE not only blessed them with a new reason to keep on, HE also blessed them with HIS presence! Isn't that just like our LORD? When we are in our darkest hour, when we are feeling the most desperate, when we feel like there is no HOPE — JESUS! Look to the shore! There, in the light of a new day, THERE HE IS! Not only did HE gently call them HIS children, HE also prepared for those tired and hungry men a wonderfully nourishing breakfast!

The truth in HIS words and HIS promises are clear. Once this wonderful SAVIOR enters our lives, **we can never go back to our old ways of life**! Oh, yes, we can stray and even lose our direction. But the JOY of KNOWING that JESUS will never leave us is wonderfully and assuredly expressed right here in this story! We can never travel beyond HIS presence. We can never stray beyond HIS reach. No matter how dark it gets, no matter how black our future or our current situation might look, JESUS is always there!

LOOK TO THE SHORE! There is a campfire burning just for us!

To comfort us, to encourage us and give us HIS nourishment! HE sent to us HIS precious HOLY SPIRIT!

This is the wonderful **comforter** that will feed us! For HE is the BREAD of LIFE. He is the LIGHT of the WORLD. He is the living WATER. And HE is our HOPE and our JOY for a better today and a brighter tomorrow! May we never, ever think it possible to go back to our old way of life. This same marvelous Savior promised us in Hebrew 13:5, "Let your life be free from the love of money, being content with what you have; for HE HIMSELF has said, I will NEVER leave you, nor will I EVER forsake you."

I truly believe those words will live with this congregation for a long time to come. During the closing prayer, I gave a personal invitation to any person who might not be sure about his or her own salvation and personal relationship with Jesus. I prayed that not one of them would leave today without the calm assurance that even should they die on this very day, they would spend eternity with Jesus in GLORY! As I ended my sermon, I assured them I would be available to any and all for prayer and personal counseling after the service.

Valentina raised her worshipful hands high and ended the service with a powerful sending-forth. Lidia gave the benediction, and then, here came the kids! After they all became well equipped to be "little missionaries," I went to the adults and prepared them also, with many remembrances of this very special Sabbath. I gave their youth director, Sergei, the last *Jesus* video we had. I am sure it will be put to great use!

As many of the people gathered for tea and snacks, I was afforded plenty of time to minister to several new believers. There is no greater joy than seeing lost souls repent of their sins and give their hearts and lives to JESUS! I was surprised at how many people wanted to pray with me about one thing or another. It was apparent from these folks' prayer requests that a great deal of pain, hurt, sorrow and uncertainty surrounded their lives. Most of them simply wanted to feel secure about their own personal salvation. What a privilege for me to pray with them on such a vital part of an individual's Christian growth and maturity. I made sure they read for themselves — out loud— some very important Scripture pertaining to "right thinking and right believing" on this essential subject of the surety of one's own personal salvation.

The Word of God confidently confirms to us this truth with expressions of peace-filled protection and assurance. For those with whom I prayed, Romans 8:34-35 and Romans 8:37-39 were the victorious and conquering Scripture verses I asked them to read out loud.

Even if you are confident about your own salvation, these wonderful verses of triumph over death, condemnation and evil should be read aloud at least once a week!

"Who is the one who condemns us? Christ Jesus is HE who died, yea, rather who was raised, and who is at the right hand of God, who also intercedes for us. Who shall separate us from the love of Christ? Shall tribulation, or distress, or persecution, or famine, or nakedness, or peril, or sword?"

"But in all of these things we are overwhelmingly conquered through HIM who first loved us. For I am convinced that neither death, nor life, nor angels, nor principalities, nor things present, nor things to come, nor powers, nor height, nor depth, nor ANY OTHER CREATED THING, shall be able to separate us from the love of God, which is in Christ Jesus our Lord."

I believe with everything that is within me that we can be — and should be — confident of our salvation.

I also believe that it is imperative for us to **"KNOW" beyond any doubt that being secure in our salvation and resting in the finished work of JESUS is the key that will unlock the door to the "abundant life" that Christ Himself promised us**.

What our Lord accomplished for us on the cross cannot

be added to. In John 5:11-13, we read about this confident and "FREE, paid-in-full" eternal life insurance program. "And the witness is this, that God has given us eternal life, and this life is in HIS SON. He who has the SON has the life; he who does not have the SON of GOD does not have the life. **These things I have written to you who believe in the name of the SON of GOD in order that you MAY KNOW that you have eternal life."**

What a joy it must be for the Lord when HE sees our faces light up with exuberant smiles as these precious words of assurance are forever settled and confirmed in our minds.

Lidia enthusiastically expressed to me that my message from God's WORD and my acting out of the Scriptures brought a great sense of personal HOPE to these spiritually hungry and, many times, confused people. She said that the words spoken today were easily understood and greatly encouraging to everyone there. Lidia and Valentina both said to me, "GOD has not abandoned our churches. HE has just begun! We will always remember, just when you think there is no HOPE; **JESUS is right there. Just look to the shore!"**

Before leaving the church, I presented Valentina with one of the beautiful crystal crosses from Ireland. She was overwhelmed to receive this gift from the wonderful people at COR! She immediately placed this meaningful cross on the open Bible on the altar.

We left the church around noon. Lidia drove three very dear friends who had attended the service and myself to the infamous Red Square. I only had one hour to do some very quick souvenir shopping for my beloved wife.

Red Square is magnificently awesome! I have no words to truly describe my feelings and emotions at seeing this fortress in person for the first time. There are miles of high, impenetrable red-bricked walls surrounding the Kremlin and the Square. Viewing the walls brings a sense of the strength of the Soviet ideology of the past. Then, walking through huge brick and stone archways leading right onto that enormous field of red paving bricks, I was overwhelmed at the astonishing sight before me!

Many times, during the chilling years of the Cold War, we saw this unique setting on television. Soviet-made tanks, military trucks, missile-carrying vehicles and erect marching soldiers proudly parading across the vast sea of red brick. To actually stand in this gigantic arena for the first time is a feeling that is difficult to describe!

These are some of the words and phrases that crowded my mind the first time I saw Red Square in 1997: history, Communism, Cold War, hatred of the West, hatred of God, bondage of people, government-controlled airwaves and publications, no free thinking, extreme suffering, persecution of believers.

On one side of the square there is a beautiful marble museum and mosque containing the remains of the founder of Communism, Vladimir Ilich Lenin. On the other side of the square sits the GUM shopping mall, whose bright signs advertising Christian Dior and Levis rival those in the West. Instead of slogans praising Lenin's legacy or exhorting hard work, banners now advertise expensive designer clothing and electronics.

How well I remember a wonderful shop (which I had visited twice before) offering beautiful pieces of crystal from the Czech Republic. Each time I am in Moscow, I choose another of their unique pieces for our collection at home.

As you walk around the Square, you see political activist everywhere, most of them carrying handmade signs praising and extolling Marxist policies and thinking from the past. People using battery-operated megaphones busily hand out Communist and socialist literature and try to chant down the Western ideal of capitalism, which seems to be winning out. Bright-shining golden "onion topped" Russian Orthodox churches surround the area. Standing majestically in the background of Red Square is the wonderful and magnificent St. Basil Cathedral. Nearly every picture of Red Square proudly highlights this great monument of Russian architecture.

Each time I set foot in Red Square I reflect on where I am standing. I am compelled to remember the great strides these people have made toward democracy, and I continue to pray for their freedom and their ability to worship in public now without fear of imprisonment and persecution. They have come a long way but there is yet a long way to go!

We're headed now for the second Methodist church that holds Saturday services. Alexei Myachin is the pastor of Moscow's Church of the Resurrection. Alexei was formerly a homeless street-person. When he found a new life in Jesus, his life was literally transformed overnight. In 1996, he was one of the first to enroll and graduate from the newly founded Moscow Methodist Seminary.

The associate pastor is a dynamic Christian leader named Sergei Nikolaev. On my first trip to Moscow in 1997, I had the privilege of staying in Sergei's home. He was a newlywed at that time, and his American wife, Deborah, was so helpful, explaining to me many of the unfamiliar Russian customs. Their romance and marriage is a true love story of two believers who dared to trust God to find the perfect mate. Sergei and Deborah have been a great help with our Leadership Institutes in Kansas City. They both are excellent interpreters, speaking fluent Russian and English. They have been tireless in their efforts to teach basic Methodist doctrines and theology at the Methodist Seminary in Moscow. They have also taken on the challenge of helping translate our wonderful 34- week program *Disciple I Bible Study* into Russian. The LORD has used these two wonderful, caring people in a magnificent way to help build a bridge of trust and love between believers from America who fall in love and enter into a marriage of oneness with believers from Russia. They are both well-

Prayer for the blessing of God's word to go forth in worship

respected by Christians and non-Christians alike. It seems to me that these two dedicated individuals are the lifeblood of strength and stability within the Methodist churches of Moscow.

The Church of the Resurrection worship services were held in the basement of a small building that seated about 70 people. Soon after we arrived there was not an empty seat available, but Pastor Alexei brought out some cushions and blankets from the missions closet. Most of the people in the congregation were at least 70 years old. Eager to participate, the elderly people came to hear me — the American lay preacher from the church with the same name as theirs.

Once I saw the group, I felt the sermon I had prepared and about which I had prayed, was very appropriate. I planned to tell the familiar story of Zaccheus in the 19th chapter of Luke, verses one through ten. The title was **"How are you going to be different when JESUS passes your way and HE enters into your home?"'**

I began by reading the text and then asking the question, "Has Jesus entered your town and passed your way to change your life?" I shared how Zaccheus, the tax collector, was so badly hated in his city that he was considered to be even worse than an evil KGB agent. Zaccheus had heard great stories about JESUS, the miracle worker. When Zaccheus found out that HE was coming to visit Jericho, the wicked tax collector decided that he MUST see HIM in person!

Pretending to be Zaccheus, I said, "I hate the direction my life is headed, and I think there is something different about this man. Maybe what people say about Him is true. If HE is the long- awaited Messiah, then HE could offer me a chance to change. Even though I am a wealthy man, my life is filled with such emptiness. Everybody hates me and I don't even like myself. I WILL GO and I WILL DO whatever it takes to SEE HIM!"

Then I acted out Zaccheus climbing into the tree to try and get a better look at HIM. I explained how the crowd must have been; so many people and all pressed in around HIM that it became impossible to see HIM clearly.

I continued, making the bold proclamation, **"What is keeping you from seeing who JESUS really is?** Is it the crowd that surrounds you? Is it your past, or your fear of persecution? Whatever it is, you must be willing to climb above your fears. You must understand that seeing JESUS as LORD with a clear and unclouded view is the only way you can have a personal, life-changing encounter with the living Messiah!"

The truth of this story brought awareness to all the people gathered in the church that **HE cares about even the worst sinner!** Jesus' sincere desire is to come and dwell in every one of our homes. HE wants to live within each of us, and to change us completely into HIS image. Jesus told Zaccheus, as well as all of us, "Hurry and come down from your past because the LORD desires to be a guest in this house today and forever!" The living Christ saw Zaccheus not as an evil tax collector, but as a man who could change into a new person with a new purpose and be given a brand-new start!

When Jesus approaches our lives as LORD and SAVIOR, five things always happen. In Luke 19, we see:

1. Verse 5; Jesus **gives us a new name** and sees us for what we can become, not for what we are. (The word "Zaccheus" actually means "pure.")

2. Verse 6; Gladness **occurs** when we see Christ for the very first time and do not hesitate to answer HIS call to obedience.

3. Verse 8; we **stop our old ways of living**. We willingly and joyfully turn away from the ways and the directions that we were headed.

4. Verse 8: We also find out that a **radical change always occurs** when we take on the image and the likeness of Christ.

5. Also in Verse 8; A **revolutionary development happens**. Zaccheus, once a terrible sinner, said he would repay **four times** what he had wrongly taken.

These five things instantly took place in the life of this lost and hated sinner. When we read and fully understand this remarkable story, we can begin to see the vastness of HIS unconditional love and the true and everlasting mercies of GOD. HE so graciously bestows upon us HIS blessings and HE goes far beyond that which we deserve. God reaches into our hearts and shows us what we can't see with our own eyes.

Can you understand what can happen to you when HE enters your life and you allow HIM to change you completely? **How are you going to be different when**

JESUS passes your way and HE enters into your life and comes to stay at your home?

Pastor Alexei closed the service with prayer. After the sermon, I was pleased and honored to share the Lord's Communion with this church. It was amazing to think that just a decade ago we would have all been sent to a Soviet gulag for four years for participating in this Holy and very sacred act in public! Praise HIS blessed Name!

I knew this was it! No more church services for another year, so I passed out everything that I had left. The older the people, I believe, the more they appreciated the "Gospel bracelets." Besides the one that I wore for the entire mission trip, there were 53 left. Even after giving mine up, I was saddened to know that about 25 people did not get one of our precious missionary tools. As a consolation, I gave each of those people four of the "cross in my pockets." We had just enough of the "I Am Loved" pins for everyone. I also left the last copies of the *4-Spiritual Laws*.

After tea and cookies, I had to say good-bye to all my dear friends once again. I promised that next year, in August 2001, we would be back with a new group of eager mission people to continue building **THE BRIDGE INTO MISSION**. Before leaving that night, I was able to present this church with the last of the crystal crosses. They were greatly appreciative of such a thing of lasting remembrance and beauty.

The trip is almost over, but the memories of what I have seen and experienced are still exploding in my mind. The vision of stronger and closer bonds with the Russian people will keep us focused. Our mission and our purpose and our goals will not fail, for they are not ours but the Lord's. Though these goals and visions are not totally understood, we will continue to build that ever-strengthening **BRIDGE INTO MISSION**.

Upon arriving back at Lidia's flat, we enjoyed our last spot of tea together. As I have done on other mission trips, I left behind two old suitcases, all of my bath and hand towels, and all of my shirts and trousers that I had brought. The suit coat and trousers that I had worn at each worship service would also be given away. It was easy to pack for the trip home — I got all my stuff into one medium-sized suitcase. I would carry home a few souvenirs for my wife, my camera, my Bible, the clothes on my back, and precious memories that will last for eternity.

DAY 17

Sunday, September 3, 2000

"Go, therefore, and make disciples of all the nations, baptizing them in the name of the Father and the Son and the Holy Spirit, teaching them to observe all that I commanded you; and lo, I AM with you always, even to the end of the age."

Matthew 28:19-20

"And beyond all these things put on love, which is the perfect bond of unity. And let the peace of Christ rule in your hearts, to which indeed you were called in one body; and be thankful. Let the word of Christ richly dwell within you; with all wisdom, teaching and admonishing one another with psalms and hymns and spiritual songs, singing with thankfulness in your heart to God. And whatever you do in word or deed, do all in the name of the LORD JESUS, giving thanks through HIM to GOD the FATHER.

Colossians 3:14-17

I shared a quick breakfast with Lidia and her family and then we were off to the airport. Because it was Sunday morning, I did not think the traffic would be bad — WRONG! The good news is, I think that either I am getting used to traffic delays or the LORD is giving me patience to endure. I pray for the latter. We arrived at the airport exit ramp with two hours to spare before my flight was to leave for GOD BLESS AMERICA.

I was horrified to see that the line of cars to the departure and arrival terminal was backed up for over two miles. These terribly frustrating lines caused a lot of short-fuse tempers to express themselves via the blasting of horns. People were abandoning their cars right in the middle of the highway. We finally managed to maneuver our way through the maze of unoccupied vehicles. We got to the parking area entrance only to find that no parking spaces were left! So we joined the crowd, adding to the mass confusion: we parked right there on the road and walked the rest of the way to the departure terminal. What a disaster! The concept of airport security took on a whole different meaning today.

Let me begin this epic by stating that before I left on this mission trip, I was warned to not fly Aeroflot Airlines by more than one person. I really should have listened to that small bit of great wisdom. But I didn't. Aeroflot was the cheapest, so that was my poor judgment's final decision.

Before we finally got to the Aeroflot terminal, I started getting pretty anxious about being late for my flight home. The relief I felt as we finally entered the terminal building quickly left me when we were told that my flight had been canceled. My first thought was, "I should have listened!" I said, "Lidia, there must be some mistake. We called before we left your flat and they told us my flight was on time." Lidia appropriately replied, "Woody, this is RUSSIA!"

The same sign that contained the message, "Aeroflot, Flight 131—CANCELLED" also read "See information desk for further instructions." I looked toward the area to which the arrow pointed and saw a very long line of people. I cast up a short "breath-prayer" and said, "Lord, please don't let that be the line that I am supposed to be standing in."

WRONG AGAIN! To my amazement, I discovered there was only **one information line** for all the Aeroflot departures and arrivals. This line that I was very reluctant to join was almost as long as the endless stream of abandoned cars we had just negotiated to get here. I asked Lidia if she would go with me and interpret, in case the **one** person behind the "choke-proof" glass did not speak English.

Forty minutes later, I finally got to ask the question, "Why has Flight 131 been cancelled, and when is the next Aeroflot flight to the U.S.?" The very terse and short-tempered lady behind the glass did speak some broken English, at least enough to cavalierly reply, "Plane no here — maybe later, plane be here!" Extremely frustrated with this ridiculous reply, I asked to speak to her boss or anyone who could give me some additional information. I have been gone from GOD BLESS AMERICA now for 17 days, and I was not in any mood to be satisfied with that response. Those words just were not going to cut it for me! The very rude, and now extremely ready for me to be gone, lady informed me that the main office for Aeroflot was located on the sixth floor.

Becoming very anxious at this point, I made my way to the elevator. I began perspiring profusely. My body was beginning to tremble. My throat was parched. After waiting for about ten very long minutes for the doors to open, I concluded that the elevator was out of order. Why should that surprise me? I have not seen a working elevator the entire time I have been here. Frustrated beyond words and now covered with sweat, I began my trudging journey, lugging all my stuff, up six flights of stairs. Was it too much to HOPE — "JESUS," that at the end of these stairs I could get some definite answers as to when I could go home?

WRONG AGAIN! When I finally reached the Aeroflot offices, I paused for a moment to let the shakes subside and catch my breath. I offered up to the LORD another quick "breath-prayer" for some **patience and a calming of my quivering body and rapidly beating heart.** By now, I was severely lacking in oxygen, and a smile or a kind word from deep within my spirit was going to be very difficult to muster up!

I knocked on the door and waited for it to open. When no one responded, my knock turned quickly into a brisk and forceful pounding. When the door finally opened, an employee of this terribly backward-thinking airline seemed bothered by the fact that I would ask such a series of intimidating questions. The reply I was about to hear was more ludicrous even than that of the lady downstairs! What I got from this lady was, "Plane has trouble. Maybe other plane be here tomorrow!"

With such a flood of valuable and reliable information coming at me all at once, I became just a bit overwhelmed. Suddenly, from out of nowhere, I heard my voice yell out, "What kind of ridiculous answer is that!" I felt faint. I was losing it. All my body functions were beginning to shut down. My throat was so dry I could not swallow. My voice began to quiver; my knees felt like Jell-O. I wanted to scream, or maybe strangle someone!

My actions up to this point were certainly not a good testimony that Christ was in total control of my life. The Lord was certainly not proud of the way I was handling this stressful situation.

At this point, I decided the best thing for my health and well-being was to just walk away, rather than wait for another preposterous reply. If I heard one more profoundly stupid statement from another Aeroflot employee, I was afraid I would risk being arrest and imprisonment in a Russian gulag! I felt as though my sentence of guilt would read, "U.S. citizen convicted of a very ugly public display of a good old-fashioned American panic attack."

I waited for my shakes to subside, and for my breathing to once again become a natural body function. I tried to employ some kind of coherent thinking. What was my next brilliant move going to be? At this point, all I was sure of was that somehow I had to find a way out of Moscow, TODAY!

This was to be my new mission! I was determined to not let my rapidly deteriorating state of mental, physical and spiritual health get the best of me. I remembered that we had flown in and out of Moscow before on Delta Airlines. So I headed back down those six flights of stairs to find the Delta Airlines area. Where was the Delta gate? Could I find Lidia, or had she left to go to church? After all, this is Sunday. These were the questions racing through my mind as I trudged down those very tiring six flights of stairs.

Halleluiah! Something was going right for a change: I found Lidia. When I told her that I was going to purchase a ticket on Delta so I could leave today, she tried to convince me that we could come back tomorrow. It did not make any sense to her for me to buy another ticket. I expressed to her as calmly as I could that it might not make sense to waste the ticket on Aeroflot, but it made less sense come back tomorrow and be told, "Plane no here — maybe tomorrow," again!

We must have asked twenty different people, all wearing airport uniforms, where the Delta gate was. No one seemed to know. My ability for competent deductive reasoning was returning, soon to be accompanied by another attack of extreme anxiety. Figuring if one airline office was located on the sixth floor, surely there was another one up there somewhere, I prayed for my composure to return. I told Lidia I was going back up those long stairs to see if I could find someone who could tell me where the Delta people are and where in the world their gate is. She assured me that she would wait downstairs to see if maybe the status of the Aeroflot flight might change.

Once again, after trudging up the six flights of stairs, I arrived at the cluster of offices where such profound and logical information was so resolutely given to me just a few moments before. But wait! There before me was a sign in English, a sign that brought a huge smile to my very fatigued face: "DELTA AIRLINES." Halleluiah!

Just think, people that speak English might be right beyond that door! I don't know when I have ever been so happy to see a door open and a smiling lady ask, "Can I help you, sir?" I did not even need an interpreter to understand this gracious and accommodating salutation!

I was able to get the very last seat on a Moscow to New York City flight that was leaving in a mere four hours. This very kind lady felt so sorry for me as I relayed the recent very entertaining and already humorous events to her. She went far beyond her obligations and routed my flight schedule all the way through to Kansas City at no extra charge. At this point, I did not care that my other ticket would be wasted nor did I care how much this one-way ticket was going to cost me. I just wanted to go home!

I labored to carry my frustrated and still shaking 52-year-old body and luggage and "stuff" back down those stairs. I found Lidia and told her the glorious news and persuade her to go on to church. She was reluctant to leave me in the airport all alone, but I insisted she go. I gave her a big hug, and as we said our farewells I told her I would see her in August of 2001 with another group of mission people.

I repeated to myself over and over that very familiar verse in Philippians, chapter 4, verse 13: "I CAN DO ALL THINGS THROUGH CHRIST WHO STRENGTHENS ME." Even though I blew my testimony to every person I came in contact with today, I SUCCEEDED! I GOT ANOTHER TICKET WITHOUT KILLING SOMEONE! I DID NOT EVEN GET ARRESTED FOR MY VERY IMMATURE TEMPER TANTRUMS! I AM GOING HOME!

As I clutched my new, life-saving Delta ticket to GOD BLESS AMERICA, thoughts of seeing my darling wife in only about 18 hours flooded my mind. I realized how very much I missed her. We have been married for only ten years, and this was the longest time we have ever been apart. I wanted so much to hear her sweet voice, but I couldn't find a working telephone. I felt peace and contentment just knowing that I would have plenty of time to call her and tell her of my flight changes, once I landed in New York.

The reality that my experience of a lifetime was fast coming to a close began to take precedence over the catastrophes of the day. I began to cry and laugh at the same time. I laughed out loud, thinking about the movie *Trains, Planes and Automobiles*. I HAD JUST LIVED IT! What an ordeal! What a total hassle! What an experience to share and remember! I was already laughing about it! I knew **now** that the Lord had prepared me to handle any airport experience imaginable!

I was determined to be the first living creature to board that plane, so I was perfectly content to stand right where I was told the Delta departure gate was going to be set up in about four hours. Right now, I was standing by some temporary roll-around counters that had Delta Airlines written on them. By the way, this was why no one knew where the Delta gate was. There was no permanent assigned gate. The Delta departure gate always gets positioned at a temporary location with roll-around portable, removable stands and fixtures.

As my sanity began to return, I realized that I was standing at the beginning of a nonexistent line at a nonexistent gate. That did not really matter to me, because I had the peaceful assurance of knowing that in only FOUR SHORT hours there would be people gathering at this very spot where HOPEFULLY the DELTA gate would be set up.

I was famished, but the security of knowing that I was to be the first passenger on that plane made my hunger pains subside. I told myself that I could eat a "real meal" in only four or five hours. I could wait to eat. I could not wait to get home!

The Delta counter right in front of me worked great as a stand up desk. I used my last four hours in Moscow to bring my journal closer to completion.

The mission trip that we had planned and prayed about for over a year was now drawing to a glorious and remarkable close. I feel this would be an appropriate time to give duly deserved credit to everyone who helped make this trip the extraordinary adventure that it was. A humble "THANK YOU TO ALL" for the generosity of the many individuals, Sunday school classes, corporations and the Missions committee at COR for their caring and loving investments in this wonderful Christ-centered expedition.

This is the list of the things that I either brought with me or were shipped over and waiting for me when I arrived in Russia for my life-changing mission trip:

1. 3,500 Russian language Adult Bibles.
2. 1,000 Russian language Children's Bibles.
3. 1,000 Romanian language Adult Bibles.
4. 1,000 large print Russian language New Testaments.
5. 43 wonderful "Presentation Bibles," published in Russian, by Kay Arthur's Precept Ministries, Inc.
6. 784 leather-thong "Gospel bracelets," made by our Sunday school classes at COR.
7. 1,000 copies of Campus Crusade for Christ's Russian language *4-Spiritual Laws.*
8. 2,000 wonderful "I Am Loved" pins, from the terrific people at Helzberg Diamonds.
9. 20 copies of the Russian language *Jesus* video.
10. 4,000 small "Smile, Jesus Loves You" hologram stickers.
11. 1,000 very meaningful "Cross in my Pocket" witness reminders.
12. Almost $800 in cash donated by many of our COR Sunday school classes. This money was spread a long way, helping many needy ministries and individuals in Moldova.
13. 15 beautiful Waterford Crystal crosses from the Irish Crystal Company of Overland Park, Kansas.

What did we get in return for our investments? The answer to this question can only be fully and accurately understood when we, ourselves, go to Glory. The LORD HIM-SELF will reveal the actual and lasting results!

I can assure all of you reading this journal that we touched the lives of many people, and gave them words of HOPE-"JESUS!" We equipped them with Bibles and many witnessing tools. We shared the Good News of Christ and HIS unconditional love with thousands of lonely and hope-lost people. We gave them a true and lasting HOPE-"JESUS!"

We spoke to people in places of high authority and to the poorest of the poor with the same life-redeeming message of peace and joy and salvation in JESUS. I promise you, these people will never forget us. We did make a difference. These poor saints, who have suffered so much and have so little, are eager to make a difference in their villages for Christ. They made us promise that we would come back. We left them our commitment that we would return.

I think about my payments. What did I receive for my 17 days of exhausting toil? How many people gave me flowers, which they had planted and cared for? How many people fed me their own precious food that was so laboriously grown?

How many apples did so many elderly saints give me because apples were all they had to share? How many "thank you for just being there" sentiments did I receive? How many kisses and hugs were given, and how many tears rained down on me as I held forgotten souls close, and prayed, and told them that they were loved? How many "I Am Loved" pins did I place on young and old alike? How many lost souls will come to Christ as a result of the *Jesus* videos we passed out?

How many children will become missionaries as they learn to use their wonderful, meaningful "Gospel bracelets"? How many lives will be forever changed through reading and understanding the *4-Spiritual Laws*? How many now know the plain and simple truths found in these *4-Laws*, because they truly understand that salvation can only come from a personal relationship with Jesus Christ? How many times will the Bibles that we gave away be read and re-read?

How many people will see the beautiful crystal crosses and think of their symbolism? How many people stood in long lines to get something from an American when they found out that we were going to be in their village the next day to preach the Gospel? How many toothless smiles did I receive from young and old as I put on them a little sticker that said, "Smile, Jesus loves you"? How many children did I have the blessed privilege to touch and lay my hands upon with prayers of blessings?

Yes, my payment has been gratefully received! I feel that I have been paid in full. The most glorious part of all, is that I can see the construction continuing as the **BRIDGE INTO MISSION** expands from the U.S. to Moscow and now on to Moldova!

Each time I return from a mission trip I find my priorities and my ideas have changed. I find myself filled with more thoughts of putting others first. I have more compassion for the lost and the poor. Whenever I see a child I smile — just because they are so beautiful and precious. I see the acceptance and the tolerance toward others that I now have. I realize the intolerance I once carried when I unjustly accused those who did not believe just like me. I am more determined than ever to never think like that again. I see the patience that is beginning to grow when things don't go my way.

Let me sum my feelings up this way: if you need more love for others, go on a mission trip. If you need more patience and tolerance, go on a mission trip. If you want to touch someone's life with an act of kindness, go on a mission trip. If you want to help fulfill the Great Commission, go on a mission trip. If you want to experience tears of happiness filling the eyes of a small child when you put a small bracelet on their precious little wrist, go on a mission trip. If you want to feel the joy of an elderly, hungry person holding your hand, looking deep in your eyes and sincerely saying, "GOD BLESS YOU," go on a mission trip. If you want to learn how to begin giving yourself to others, go on a mission trip. If you want to witness God's Word being lived out, day by day as HE intended it to be lived, go on a mission trip.

But how many people have the opportunity or the physical strength or the finances to travel abroad? How many people are willing, but just don't know where to begin? How many people, because of their jobs, just cannot undertake a trip of thousands of miles and many days to tell someone in a faraway land about the love of Christ?

Each and every one of us can go! Each and every one of us must go!

You don't have to be a full-time foreign missionary to be an effective full-time missionary! The profound truth is we all can become valuable missionaries right in our own villages! You don't have to travel around the world to tell your next-door neighbors about Jesus or invite them to your church. You don't have to go very far to find time to help someone less fortunate than yourself. We can all give a smile and a kind word of encouragement to the discouraged. We can all visit a local nursing home and just offer a smile to the lonely people while just listening to them. We can all be more like Christ at our workplace, and even on our drive to work. We all can learn to be more forgiving when we are treated badly. We can all say a kind word to someone who might not be so kind.

We all can become HIS instruments for HIS mission, whatever or wherever HE might lead.

When you are having a really bad day and everything is rotten, remember one of my "Woodyisms." Say to yourself, "My worst day in GOD BLESS AMERICA is better than the people of Russia's best day could ever possibly be!" Suddenly things don't seem so bad.

My main goal for this trip was that JESUS be glorified in everything that was done. HIS name was made known to many. HE did direct our every step. I asked the question, "Was HE truly glorified?" I will let the LORD be the judge of that. I truly believe that this was HIS TRIP! I am so thankful that HE chose me to step beyond my comfort zone and go on HIS mission.

Why don't you plan on going on your own mission trip wherever the Lord might be leading you? Then you can see for yourself the glorified and risen Lord bringing "mission" to live within your own life! Start that trip right now, wherever you are.

Remember, everyone can build a **BRIDGE INTO MISSION**!

I want to end this book with a verse from the Word that I think pretty well sums up my thoughts about mission and this wonderful Christ-centered trip.

"And to know the love of Christ which surpasses all knowledge, that you may be filled up to all the fullness of God. Now to HIM who is able to do exceeding abundantly beyond all that we ask or think, according to the power that works within us, to HIM be the glory in the church and in Christ Jesus to all generations forever and ever. Amen." Ephesians 3:19-21

"THE BEGINNING"
(Now, the first step is up to you.)

WHAT'S NEXT?

Prayer — Preparation — Perseverance!

After finishing the rough draft of this book, I still felt like something was missing. What was I leaving out? After much prayer I felt the Lord was leading me to direct my thoughts toward helping others *take that first bold step in building* **A BRIDGE INTO MISSION.**

What came next was the idea of formulating a clear and comprehensive timeline type of approach for all the preparations necessary to plan a mission trip. Let's just call this last part of the book "A Complete and Comprehensive List of Construction-Instructions."

In many ways, a mission trip must be looked at like every other adventurous journey we decide to undertake. One of the best ways to be assured of a successful mission, regardless of where your travel might lead, is to be prepared to persevere through prayer and persistence! We must pray while we plan and we must do our homework for the unexpected. Preparing for a mission trip of any kind is a huge task. At each stage of planning, every detail must be addressed and properly understood. My hope is that by following this list of "Construction-Instructions," much of the stress and frustration that usually accompanies such a monumental task can be avoided. My prayer is the Lord will bless you in every area of your preparations. May these efforts result in an encouraging, positive, fruitful and Christ-centered mission expedition for you or your group.

The following information is a combination of what I have experienced and learned from the school of hard knocks, and what I have gleaned from different seminars my wife and I have attended on mission work. Most of the information for this wide-ranging list of necessary preparations was gathered from notes taken and printed materials we received when attending a weekend seminar called "Volunteer in Mission Leadership Training." These UMVIMs, as they are called, are organized and sponsored by the United Methodist Church. My grateful thanks must go to Barb Stone, who has led these valuable educational seminars for several years. Barb has given me permission to use UMVIM's basic "Guidelines for Proper Preparation." She has also allowed me to make changes as I saw the need. This information is directed toward, and more focused on, a foreign mission with emphasis on evangelism. We will further examine the wonderful UMVIM program, and discover why it has become so popular for people of all faiths as we progress.

Mission Concepts for Consideration

Before we can begin our mission, there are some key things that I believe should be considered that will greatly contribute to the overall success of any Christ-centered mission trip.

First of all, I believe it is very important to understand that there is a great difference between the theories of "*missions*" work versus "mission" work. Probably a number of you have noticed that the book was titled, **A Bridge into Mission** — not *Missions*. I recently met a wonderful pastor that I would like to quote. I think what he said can help illustrate the difference in these two very important concepts. Pastor Jeremy Bassett, formerly of Cape Town, South Africa, serves as the Director of Mission and Community Outreach at the Church of the Servant in Oklahoma City,

Oklahoma. He is not only serving the Lord by leading this great church's mission programs, he is also working on his Ph.D. in the study of Christian Mission. Jeremy Bassett made a profound statement about fundamental Christian theology that I will always remember. He said, "Our Lord's command was for us to do HIS **Mission. There is only one Great Commission.** When we try to add to **HIS Mission** and make it *missions,* we have a tendency to get things out of focus and we can easily be distracted. If we are to be an effective witness for Christ in our mission efforts, we MUST be about **HIS MISSION** — not *missions."*

Having said all this, we should, however, clarify that even though there is only **one mission**, there can be several different kinds of mission trips that one can focus on. When thinking about what type of mission trip to become involved with, there are basically three different goals or areas of mission concentration that can be examined and explored.

Areas of Mission Concentration

1. Medical mission—assisting or being a part of a team of pharmacists, dentist, doctors and nurses whose main objective is to show the love of Christ through the field of medicine. Working side by side with local doctors and nurses, teaching and instructing them in the latest technologies, is the main focus. Through their dedicated efforts, they are also reaching out to those who desperately need healing and medical assistance.

2. Building or Construction mission — being part of a team of workers who feel the call to serve Christ with their hands. Coordinating and leading a team to assist and work alongside the local church people in the construction of housing, churches, or other needed buildings.

3. Evangelism and Discipleship mission — leading or working as a part of a team of other fellow believers whose main objective is sharing the Good News of Christ

and HIS never-changing message in any part of the world where it is needed. That is everywhere! I believe the mission team should exhibit much prayer should be devoted to working directly with the pastors and members of the already established local churches. We must follow as closely as possible the duties and the purposes of the early church. The objectives ordained by Christ are explained and set forth in the second chapter of Acts, beginning with verse 41. We must be continually devoted to preaching and teaching, fellowship, breaking of bread, and prayer.

Everyone who has heard the call from the Lord and feels led to become involved in mission work must remember, "**A MISSION TRIP IS NOT A VACATION.**" The 12 disciples took very seriously their individual call and the command from our Lord. All but one gave their lives in a martyr's death because they were not afraid to follow that call. Our mission goal is simple but it is not easy. Let us never forget HIS command and the powerful words behind the Great Commission, found in Matthew 28:18-20, "All authority has been given to ME in heaven and on earth. Go therefore and make disciples of all nations, baptizing them in the name of the Father and the Son and the Holy Spirit, teaching them to observe all that I commanded you; and lo, I am with you always, even to the end of the age."

What do I need to do to begin?

I think the first thing that everyone needs to consider is how to become active and get involved in your own local churches mission program. If your church doesn't have one — start one. Work side by side with your pastor or the person who has been assigned to direct the mission work. Decide what area of concentration your church's people could be most effective in; i.e., medical, construction or evangelism.

More About UMVIM

Let me share a great way to not only get involved in mission work but to also become properly trained as a team leader at the same time. Several years ago, the people involved with the General Board of Global Ministries of the United Methodist Church realized that the world could be reached for Christ far more effectively if they could train and equip the average layperson with the tools necessary to become a missionary for a week or two during the year. It takes almost two very costly years just to prepare one full-time missionary and his family to be properly equipped to serve in the foreign mission field. It was discovered, however, that most everyone could give up one week of his or her vacation time to serve the Lord through mission work. Through this marvelous vision the concept was formed to create UMVIM offices strategically placed throughout the United States. Each office has trained and qualified staff members who serve the Lord by helping people of all faiths know what mission work is all about. Each UMVIM staff member is part of a team of dedicated workers directing the efforts behind the very successful training program the United Methodist Church calls "Volunteers in Mission."

Even though "Volunteers in Mission" is led and sponsored by the United Methodist Church, the seminars are available to everyone, regardless of church affiliation. I truly believe the weekend seminar that is offered twice a year in most areas of the U.S. should be seriously considered by anyone interested in going on a foreign mission trip, and should be **mandatory** for anyone wanting to lead a group. For more information on very educational UMVIM meetings in your area, visit the United Methodist Volunteer In Mission website at http://gbgm-umc.org/connections/vimpages.html.

I am very proud to be a part of the ever-growing evangelical United Methodist movement. I believe that this great denomination is now back in step, and is once again doing serious work for the Lord. The great founder of the Methodist church, John Wesley, had a passion for mission. Today, this same message of hope and salvation in Christ and Christ alone is being boldly proclaimed by literally thousands of UMVIM volunteers everywhere. Many a UMVIM warrior for Christ has given up a vacation, paid all of their own expenses, and traveled throughout the world to serve our Lord, not only by their actions, but also with HIS words of hope and the promise of eternal life as well.

The New Testament instructs those who would be followers of Jesus to feed the hungry, clothe the naked, give shelter to the homeless, heal the sick, care for the widows and orphans, and nurture the children. We are told that Jesus came in order that we might be able to tear down walls of hostility that divide, and HE will build bridges of understanding. We are called, wherever we are in this big world, to love all of God's creation and to demonstrate that love with Christ-like actions. This is the authority that drives each team member involved with UMVIM training.

I truly believe that when we put our faith into actions we become powerful witnesses for the cause of Christ in the world that surrounds us. We also demonstrate the very heart and soul of our Christian calling. Mission work is not just something that we do in our spare time after we have reached our personal goals. Our task driving the mission must always be secondary to our main purpose — **sharing the love of Jesus in a practical way anywhere and everywhere we can**. This is what makes Christianity different from the rest of the world's religions, and must always be our most important purpose. Through "Volunteers in Mission" not only does every person in every church have the opportunity to lift up Christ in everything we do, we also serve the Lord by giving ourselves to others the way Christ did. When we are obedient and answer the call to serve HIM, immediately our lives become much richer. We are filled with a new purpose — HIS purpose — through faith-based living. We know that when we reach out in this way, using what God has given us in the service of others, we, too, can share in the life-transforming experience the Apostle Paul describes to us in Romans 12:1-2.

Guidelines for Basic Preparations

I think one of the best ways to develop an interest for mission work in your local church is by educating and raising the awareness of actual needs that can be met through your mission efforts. This can be accomplished by recruiting volunteers who have participated in past mission experiences. Listening to a moving story of actual events, needs that were miraculously met, and how it was accomplished can go a long way to motivate a group for foreign mission work.

Begin by Deciding the Basics:

1. Select possible locations and identify some potential projects.
2. Decide on an area of concentration; i.e., construction, medical, or evangelism.
3. Contact the conference or jurisdictional UMVIM coordinator for a list of approved projects, or access this information at their website — http://gbgm-umc.org/vim.
4. Confirm with the hosting church that a team of inexperienced but willing workers would be welcomed.
5. Ensure that the project selected fits the gifts, talents and skills of those participating.
6. Establish potential dates that are agreeable to both the sending and the hosting church.
7. Enlist your pastor to give some encouraging words promoting the proposed mission trip.
8. Provide your church members with a sign-up sheet handout that contains specific information.
9. Announce the date for the first preliminary planning meeting.

Selection of the Team Leader

Pray for the Lord to give the group HIS keen discernment and wisdom in selecting the group team leader. This will be one of the most important decisions the group will make. Handle it with prayer! The goal of the team leader should always be to display a servant's attitude, and to maintain a well-balanced mission team in which everyone can participate, using his or her gifts for the purpose of glorifying Christ.

Essential Qualities of a Team Leader:

1. Commitment to mission work of the church with a spirit of humility and Christ-like humbleness.
2. Previous experience as team member or co-leader.
3. One who can exhibit great patience, and remain tolerant, flexible and open in the face of sometimes extreme difficulties. Maintain a good sense of humor, no matter what!
4. A mature Christian who has a solid Bible-based foundation of what it means to be a disciple of Jesus. Someone who can encourage the team to walk by faith.
5. Ability to make decisions in a positive and constructive way, including all the team members in the process.
6. Ability to organize, share and delegate responsibilities in a spirit of serving Christ.
7. Exhibit a caring attitude, maintaining a culturally sensitive spirit.
8. Go with an attitude of "I want to work with you," never with the attitude of "I will do for you or I will do to you."
9. Considers everyone on the team to be a vital member of the body of Christ. Allows everyone to have responsibilities and sees that each member uses his or her gifts to the glory of God.

Create a Time-Line
9 to 12 Months Before Team Leaves

It is crucial that the sending church early on establishes and maintains clear communication with the hosting church or churches. Determine the best form of communication between the sending church and the hosting church(es). Consider and plan for additional costs, and advise the hosting church of your plans for reimbursement. Make every effort to ensure that honest communication occurs in a timely manner. You must **receive a formal letter of invitation** from the hosting church for the purpose of securing travel documents and visas for all of the group members from the sending church.

Request the following information from the hosting church

1. Figure the anticipated costs of housing, meals/food arrangements, and transportation costs. Keep in mind that the people you will be serving and working with are very poor. Make arrangements with the pastors of the hosting church, and be sure that it is explained that the hosting families will be compensated for the food that is consumed by the members of the sending church. In truth, most people would give you their last piece of bread before they would ever complain. We usually figure about $10 American per day per person. If they will not take the money, tell them they can put it in their church's offering plate. This way it gets them off the hook, and they can decide what is the best way to use the money that is offered.

2. Maximum number of team members that can be accommodated by the hosting church. Keep in mind that one of the biggest obstacles you will have to deal with is local transportation. We generally do not take more than 10 people.

3. Obtain and distribute information on the country's customs and cultural expectations.

4. Make sure you have qualified and honest interpreters. Our church has a policy that all interpreters must be believers. We have found those interpreters that do not

know Jesus have a very difficult time translating Christian phrases; i.e., God's Word, being saved, born again, sovereignty of God, authority of the believer.

5. Inquire regarding appropriate gifts to offer to the community and to the hosting families.

6. Covenant with the both sending and hosting teams to pray for one another.

Other Travel Essentials

1. Learn about any recommended immunizations. Usually, your local health department can inform you of any shots you will need and provide them at a reduced rate.

2. Secure temporary international health insurance. We use Wallach & Company, Inc., of Middleburg, Virginia. We feel this firm offers the best value and is very experienced. Their phone number is 1-800-237-6615. Usually the rates are about $5 per day per person.

3. If your church decides to offer any scholarships, fundraising activities and events should be planned and scheduled.

4. **Receive formal letter of invitation from hosting churches.**

5. Decide if your team wants to send over Bibles. How many will be needed and to where should they be shipped for safekeeping until your group arrives?

6. Transportation details and tentative airline schedules should be obtained, with all reservations confirmed in writing.

Maintaining your Timeline

Timelines are very important to the sending church. They should be established early in the planning stages of every mission trip. But remember that when you arrive in the hosting church's country, everything changes. You are no longer on your time schedule, but theirs. Being rigid and inflexible will destroy not only your testimony, but your mission purpose is also greatly compromised. You must ALWAYS maintain a teachable spirit as well as keeping a good sense of humor even in the face of a seeming disaster! In spite of what you may have hoped to accomplish but didn't, Jesus is still **always in control**. If this is truly the Lord's mission, then anything and everything that you do must done in the name of Jesus, even if it means throwing all your plans and preparations in the garbage can. Many a mission trip's well thought out plans and expectations seem to have had a disastrous beginning. Then only a few days into the trip, those same aborted plans, by HIS divine providence, turn into a glorious way of birthing a total trust in Christ for HIS ultimate purpose. Our goal should be to illuminate to everyone that God's plans are never a failure and HIS ultimate purpose is always accomplished. Being flexible and tolerant are two very important traits that every team member must always keep in the front of their minds.

Additional Plans

1. Establish departure and return dates.
2. Set deadlines for forms and money to be turned in to the team leader.
3. Set dates for team training.
4. Investigate the possibility of the team leader and several of the team members attending a UMVIM training session in your area.
5. At one of the very first organizational meetings assign each team member a session to which they will bring the devotional and the scripture reading.

Prepare a Budget

1. Use a record book to enter all expenditures. Assign a team treasurer who will be responsible for keeping track of all monies.
2. Project all fixed costs. Airfare and local transportation are always the biggies.

3. Next largest is housing accommodations in the hosting church's country.

4. Estimate costs for postage, tips, departure taxes, bottled water, overweight baggage fines, sightseeing excursions, and any meals that the hosting church will not provide.

5. A host gift from your local sending church to the hosting church. We have found great success in having some of the small groups in our church make colorful worship banners, altar coverings for the pulpit, a covering for the communion table, or even a beautiful chalice inscribed with the name of the sending church and the dates of the trip.

6. Plan to spend about $50 to $75 putting together a comprehensive first-aid kit.

7. Offer to pay for the farewell fellowship meal with the hosting church, but let them plan it.

8. The team leader should research and find someone in your local area who would be willing to attend each training session and teach some basic language skills. This can sometimes become very costly, so fees should be agreed upon before the first meeting. I have found that even when you butcher the language, the fact that you tried means a great deal to the hosting church members.

3-6 Months Before Team Leaves

Keep the communication with the hosting church a top priority. Continue your covenant prayer vigil on both sides of the ocean. Plan and present monthly informational meetings at your church; more frequent meetings are good. Choose a verse of scripture that you feel best illustrates your mission goals and have the group repeat the verse at every meeting. It is a great idea to plan an ethnic dinner, inviting all the husbands and wives of the sending church's team. Try to recruit someone from the area to which you will be traveling to prepare the foods and explain their cultural significance.

Team Assignments

By now, the team leader should know the varying gifts and talents of the sending church team, and he or she should make specific job assignments for **everyone** going. Most probably, the medicine man and the finance person are already busy at their specific tasks. However, each team member must be willing to take on anything asked of him or her by the team leader. Remember, everyone must strive to maintain a teachable spirit and a good sense of humor, at all costs! Following are some suggestions for titles and job descriptions for the different team members. You can change them and add to them as your mission plans progress. The most important task is to see that **everyone has been given a purpose** and everyone is using his or her gifts to glorify the Lord. Big egos and pious pride are not part of this list, so leave them at home.

I think it should be noted that if one of your team members happens to be a pastor or your preacher, the role and the participation of his or her leadership should be discussed and decided upon before the trip begins. A pastor can be a great asset to the team, but I truly feel that the proper function of a pastor on a mission trip should be one of support and encouragement for the entire team. This really means that a mission trip should be a time for the pastor to **lead by listening** and cheering others on, helping each team member become a leader as well.

1. **The Devotional leader/Spiritual advisor** — should plan, prior to departure, a morning and evening devotional for every day your team is serving in the hosting country. This person should be mature enough in the Lord that they can help direct the spiritual course of the mission team and should also know HIS Word and how to use it effectively in difficult moments.

2. **The Team Photographer** — responsible for planning and taking group and individual photos and maintain-

ing documentation of where and when they were taken. We suggest that the team photographer bring a digital camera, so if you find a place with email access, the latest photos can be sent back to your home church.

3. **Administration/Finance/Coordination** — this responsibility should be assigned in one of your first group meetings. The finance person is responsible for tracking all budgeted expenditures and keeping the team aware of money spent. We have found that if you are going to an area where they will only accept crisp new un-circulated currency, the money should be equally divided and each person should carry some of the money. These three functions can be assigned as three individual jobs if the team leader feels the need.

4. **Medicine Person** — responsible for the team's medical forms, immunization records, and purchasing and maintaining the team's first-aid kit.

5. **Historian/Librarian** — will keep a group journal while preparing for the trip as well as during the trip. This person will also research and copy articles found in your local paper and other periodicals to keep the team abreast of conditions in the hosting country.

6. **Musician** — will prepare and lead team members in singing several songs in the hosting country's tongue. Chooses and obtains the team's music. The musician should also be willing to lead the singing if necessary at the hosting church.

7. **Tour Guide** — will explore and suggest visits to important cultural sites in the host country. Present brochures and possible places to visit for the group for final decisions. Make arrangements for the tickets. Have a keen sense of direction. Help with the team scrapbook.

8. **Creative Ministry Concepts** — You may be someone who might not be gifted for any of the above tasks. The person in this position can help create a new awareness in each individual's spirit to step out with a sense of bold-

ness and bring new ideas of ministry for the group to explore. This person can also do research on the history of existing churches in the host country and prepare the team for any cults they might encounter while on the mission trip.

More Travel Essentials

1. Provide ample time for obtaining passports, visas, and work permits where needed. For those who will need to obtain an original birth certificate, plan on waiting about six months to get a passport.
2. If your trip is a medical mission, pursue and obtain verification of professional credentials for serving in the host country (i.e., physician's license).
3. Remind team members to get the recommended immunizations and keep all immunization documents in your passport pouch.
4. Transportation details. Who will be picking you up at the airport? How you will be transported to your hotel or to your hosting families' homes?
5. Determine procedures for transporting non-personal baggage; i.e., tools or equipment.
6. Enlist someone on the team to research sightseeing excursions in your down time and make the necessary arrangements for transportation and any costs involved.
7. Make sure you have a clear understanding of host expectations on both ends.
8. It should be stressed that every team member should plan on and be capable of carrying all their own luggage. **If you can't carry it, don't take it!**

Emergency Preparation (Team Leader)

1. Be aware of any medical facilities in the area.
2. Know the health needs of team members (allergies, chronic conditions, etc.), and the person to contact in case of emergency.

3. Educate yourself regarding medical procedures in host locale.
4. Secure American embassy and consulate locations and phone numbers.
5. Have an evacuation plan in case of severe weather, social upheaval, medical emergency, etc.
6. Be sure that the team member putting together your first-aid kit knows some basic first aid. This team member will be the medicine person for the entire mission experience.

Witnessing tools to Secure

I maintain that this should definitely be a part of every mission trip, regardless of your area of concentration. Many people do not feel comfortable sharing their testimony verbally. Many people who might consider going on a mission trip do not think that they are qualified because they are not well equipped in basic Bible knowledge. There is a very effective way to overcome these obstacles. The following three items are only a suggestion, but I believe they can be very valuable witnessing tools as your team begins to step out in faith and use them. They not only will build a stronger Christ-like boldness for all the team members, they also help your team members realize just how easy and painless it is to be a witness for Christ. Most important is their purpose: to gently and lovingly help spread the love of Jesus without the panic that many feel when sharing their faith with a stranger. There are many great witnessing tools that are lightweight and fairly inexpensive. Make sure every team member carries a few of each. Instruct the less bold members of your team by role-playing how to distribute the items to the people they will be serving as well as people on the streets.

1. **The *Jesus* video** — You can obtain this wonderful mission tool directly from The Jesus Film Project, by calling 1-800-432-1997. This Christ-inspired video is produced in over 600 different languages and in several dif-

ferent VCR formats. Be sure to tell them what language you need and to which country you will be going. This is one of the greatest means of opening doors to evangelism that I have ever witnessed. Don't worry that the host country may not have an ample supply of VCRs. You will be surprised! The Lord will provide a way! Ten or more of these wonderful films will be mailed to you for about $10 each. The price if fewer than ten videos are purchased is a bit higher. It is estimated that every film sent out into the mission field produces more than a thousand fold harvest of souls for the Kingdom.

2. **The *4-Spiritual Laws* —** These blessed witnessing tools are available directly from a company called Integrated Resources, Inc. They are, I believe, by far the best-produced witnessing tracts available today. The pure and simple message of the Good News of Christ is not hyped or over-done, nor is the message of salvation and hope in Christ and Christ alone diluted in any way. You can call 1-800-729-4351, and specify the language needed. They come in packages of 100 for about $0.25 each.

3. **The "I AM LOVED" Pins —** These wonderful little tools can be obtained from the generous people at the Helzberg Diamonds website. They are usually free to any group requesting them. You can access this site at www.iamloved.org. Click on the "order" button and follow the step-by-step instructions. If you do not have access to the Internet, you can send your request in writing to Helzberg Diamonds, I Am Loved Program, 1825 Swift, North Kansas City, MO 64116. Please mention your organization and explain your purpose. These small but very powerful buttons are available in nine different languages. What a beautiful and practical way to show people of a different tongue and a different culture that Jesus loves them! Even though these little buttons were not originally intended for use as witnessing tools, they have become a very effective instrument of

evangelism. Your entire team should wear them wherever you go in whatever you are doing. Always be ready to pin them on anyone you see that might need a smile. I usually spot a little child and bend way down, pointing to mine, and then make a display out of reaching into my pockets and getting one for them. That is generally all it takes. It amazes me that the people you are serving generally don't want to put the pin on themselves, but will hold out their shirts or their coats and point to your button with a huge smile of appreciation. Something so small given in the name of Jesus will show HIS never-ending and unconditional love in a practical way. Be sure to carry plenty with you and be prepared for a great deal of excitement when you begin to pin them on the people. What a joy it is to write about these rich and rewarding experiences. I promise you, the huge smiles and the gracious nod of grateful appreciation will stay with you for a long time to come! To old and young alike these simple buttons will make a profound impact on the lives of the people you meet.

Preparing the Team: 1 to 2 months before departure

Continue communication with hosting church. By now, both teams should have a good idea of their mission goals or tasks they hope to accomplish. Continue in covenant prayer relationships for your individual team members and the individuals that you will be serving at your hosting church.

More Team Training and Education

1. Emphasize cultural sensitivity and awareness of customs of the hosting location. Team members should begin to prepare for the cultural shock of restroom facilities, food and eating customs, sleeping accommodations, and bathing procedures.
2. Begin to memorize the tenth chapter of Luke, verses 1-

12. We must remember, what ever we are served, no matter how horrible it might smell or taste, we are to eat whatever is set before us! You don't have to eat it all but you should at least make an attempt.

3. If possible, invite a native or previous missionary to share with your team how the sending team should approach and address some of the foreign religions and possibly hostile cults in the host country.

4. You must address the different moral values and some of the unusual traditions of the hosting country. Acceptable dress and correct behavior at all times will be a reflection of the values that we place on our Christian witness to the hosting community.

5. **Every team member should avoid tobacco or any form of alcohol, even if it is offered.**

Communicate with Hosting Church and verify final arrangements
(Team Leader)

You are now getting down to the time when all the loose ends need to be sewn up. Never assume that a detail not decided upon before you leave will work out after you arrive. Details left undone are a problem waiting to happen. Have a clear understanding of the sending church's goals for what your group hopes to accomplish, and the hosting church's expectations of the needs that will be prayerfully. Each team member should be warned about making **ANY** promises to a hosting church or a hosting family. This is a very good way for misunderstanding to occur and many a mission trip has lost its focus by team members' good intentions coupled with an insincere promise. All promises of any kind or the offering of invitations should be cleared by the officials in your home church as well as the home conference. Never give money to a hosting family without the prior approval of the entire team.

1. The team leader should contact the hosting country's

embassy in Washington, D.C. All necessary arrangements to secure any needed documents should be compiled and forwarded to the embassy to obtain all proper visas. Be sure **all your correspondence** with the embassy is done by traceable **overnight mail**. **Preaddressed and prepaid overnight envelopes** must be included. It is very helpful to develop a good relationship with the particular person who has been assigned to your file.

2. Be sure that lodging/sleeping and eating accommodation details are all finalized.

3. Identify special dietary requests and health needs.

4. Send the demographics of all team members to your hosting church. Include names, ages, and gender. Note those traveling with a spouse, and give a brief testimony of every team member.

5. Discuss site preparation upon arrival and projected tools/equipment/building materials that will be needed.

5. Confirm transportation plans and shuttle arrangements.

6. Confirm with hosting church joint worship opportunities.

7. Secure the funds you will take in the best form and currency. (If you are taking American dollars, you should get almost new, or preferably, un-circulated bills from your bank.)

8. The team leader should verify that all plane tickets have correct names, times, and departure and arrival information. Make copies of everyone's passport and visas. It is a good idea for the team leader to carry photocopies of each and to leave your church office a copy of them also.

9. The team leader should write a letter to your U.S. congressman explaining the mission trip and your purpose. This letter should also ask the congressman to send you a simple letter stating the full name of each of your team members and asking that the hosting country extend every courtesy while your group is traveling in that country.

10. The team leader should also purchase prepaid long distance phone cards and make sure that they are accepted in the country to which you will be traveling. Be sure you know the country's access code and how to use your phone cards before you depart.

11. The team leader should be sure that each person has copies of his passport picture page and any visas, placing a copy in every suitcase brought on the trip. Each person should also carry a photocopy of both passport and visas at all times. In case a passport is lost, this will make it much easier to obtain a new one.

12. The team leader should help plan a dedication and sending forth service for your team in conjunction with the pastor.

13. The team leader should also decide, with your pastor's advice and suggestions, what gifts are to be given to the hosting churches from the sending churches.

14. The team leader should advise the team members to make or purchase a small house gift for each of the hosting families with whom you will be staying.

2 to 3 Weeks Before Team Leaves
Finalize All Travel Plans

All airline tickets should be kept in a safe by the team leader and not given out until the day of or the day before your departure. Coordinate, with your pastor, the sending off service. This is a very special time for the team members and a special time to unite the sending church in covenant prayer each day for the team.

In final communication
with host church, confirm:

1. Travel arrivals and meeting arrangements.
2. Exact nature of work to be done (any changes).
3. Materials accessible as planned (using local merchants whenever it is possible).

4. Housing arrangements finalized.
5. Currency exchange.

Arrange to pack all non-personal items

1. Tools, team supplies, Bible School materials (if appropriate), gifts, medicine (if appropriate)
2. Make copies for travel of the complete packing list of everything you are taking for customs clearance.
3. An excellent idea is to have each team member scout out the Dollar General stores or discount houses in your area for inexpensive reading glasses and small eyeglass repair kits. Make a witness out of your search by asking to speak to the manager and tell him or her why you are asking for a discounted price. Reading glasses are an invaluable item that cannot easily be obtained in many areas. The small eyeglass repair kits can usually be purchased for around a dollar. Again, this is something that cannot be found in many countries. These items will pay royal dividends for many years to come.

As the Team Travels
Team Leader Reminders

1. The team leader should carry the list of all participants, appropriate travel documents, i.e., letter of invitation to be used at Customs.
2. Continue team building, especially if your team arrives from various geographical locations.
3. Remind your team of their role as servants in God's mission, and as guests in the host locale.

Individual Reminders

1. Remind team members to carry their Bibles with them at all times, using travel time to read and to meditate. Read and reread Acts, chapter 2 and Luke, chapter 10.
2. Begin individual journals, listing your hopes and your individual goals.

3. Keep all medications in original containers.
4. Carry identification card (include: host information, personal and medical information).

When Your Team Arrives

1. Greet hosts at port of entry. Remember that everyone is tired and probably a bit tense. It is the team leader's responsibility to prepare all the team members for just such a situation. Keep a good sense of humor at all costs!
2. Everyone should help, however, loading luggage into transportation vehicle(s).
3. Attend pre-arranged onsite orientation presented by the hosting church and celebrate new possibilities for Christian community.
4. Notify embassy/consulate that your team is in country if appropriate, and if directed.
5. Please remember you begin your mission trip as soon as you leave home. You will have plenty of opportunities to share your faith and tell your purpose on the way to your destination, so take plenty of witnessing tools and tracts on the airplane or whatever means of transportation you are taking. Being prepared to tell those you encounter about the mission will go a long way in preparing your heart and your spirit for what the Lord has in store. Chances are there will be people on the plane who could possibly live where you are going, and your testimony can prepare their hearts for HIS message.

Team Leader with Host Leader

1. Communicate frequently with host that all plans and arrangements are working.
2. Transfer project funds, and funds for in-country expenses, if not previously sent.
   Note: remember to request receipts for all money spent.

Team with Community

1. Ensure that the team is relating spiritually and positively with host church.
2. Ensure that the community is working alongside the hosting church members.
3. Include the local Christian community in worship and witness to celebrate what Christ has done for you.
4. Each team member should be aware of the joy of mission and the joy of cultural diversity.
5. Be prepared to share faith experience(s) if requested.
6. Pastors and members of the sending team should be prepared to preach if asked.
7. Include your host and local people from the hosting church in some of the devotionals for the entire group.

Being a Team

1. Provide time for daily devotionals and team meetings.
2. Each team member should always celebrate the uniqueness of each and every day.
3. Each team member should radiate Christ's love in thought and action.
4. Remember that you are guests in their country, and you are there to SERVE!
5. You should also remember that you are there to lift up Jesus in everything you do.
6. You must keep a good sense of humor and remain relaxed, tolerant, and flexible at all times.
7. Adapt to different living conditions, foods and cultural shocks with an attitude of SERVICE to our LORD and HIS people.
8. Each day should begin with prayer and end in a time of group sharing and prayer.
9. Include a time for team processing at the end of each day.
10. Encourage reflection upon the culture in light of a new experience in Christian service.

11. Team members should be informed and involved as changes occur.
12. If construction work is being done, adhere to local construction codes. If yours is a medical mission, follow World Health Organization guidelines regarding shipping medical supplies near or beyond expiration dates.
13. Each team member should be warned to not draw a lot of attention to a prize possession or a family heirloom that belongs to the hosting family. They will try to give it to you.

Daily Work-Safety Reminders

1. Give work assignments to team members based on skills, knowledge and willingness to learn.
2. Coordinate cultural opportunities with hosting church.
3. Set apart time for cultural and historical sharing of local sights, if appropriate. Remember, building relationships are as significant as completion of tasks.
4. You should expect full cooperation with all team members.
5. Be considerate of others.
6. Be sensitive to cultural dress.
7. Be willing to listen ... really listen!

Spiritual Growth

1. Be willing to learn, to grow, and to stretch your own horizons without condemnation.
2. Expect and pray for a wonderful Christian experience. Read Romans 8:28.
3. Be open and responsive to ways you can step out of your comfort zone and touch someone's life in a tangible way.
4. Pray and be aware of how God is changing you each day as you are being conformed into HIS likeness. Be aware that HIS special strength will be granted unto you every hour of every day that you saturate yourselves in HIS Word and do HIS Work.

5. Allow Christ to work in and through you. Recognize that it is Jesus who is using you to reach His people. All work and every effort must be performed for HIS glory.

Before Departure

1. Include a time for mutual assessment of the experience from both sides.
2. Invite the host to share a written assessment of the mission.
3. Make sure all expenses have been reimbursed and review expenditures and receipts with host.
4. Settle incidental expenses that occurred during the mission trip.
5. Plan with host a time for good-byes. Include a time of celebration and a final worship service. This is something that is generally planned by the hosting church on the sending church's behalf.
6. Accept and give gifts graciously, as this is a time of celebration and heartfelt bonding.
7. Establish ways to stay in touch with the host community. Be sure to leave your host church plenty of money for return postage.
8. Review with your host the departure time, transportation and procedures for the airport.

En route Home

1. Distribute and later collect team member evaluations.
2. Remind team that this should be a time to finish journals and spend time alone with the Lord. Each person should write down and be prepared to share with the group at your first reunion meeting the one thing they learned that will never be forgotten. Maybe you can come up with your own "Woodyism."
3. Remind the team that their family members have not had the same experience and to be sensitive to levels of enthusiasm or lack of enthusiasm.

4. Be sensitive to powerful emotions as the group returns home and disbands. It might take a week or two for team members to assimilate back into their home culture. The team leader should prepare each team member for a time of withdrawal and maybe even some depression. It can be quite a shock when one returns home to hot showers, clean and safe running water, warm and safe surroundings, clean homes and soft carpet. Each of these feelings should be carefully explained. For some people, returning from their first mission trip can be a scary and depressing experience, so BE PREPARED!

After the Team Returns Home

1. Send a short letter of appreciation from all the team members to the hosting church. Include your assessments of the trip and some photos.
2. Request that all team members make duplicate photos to share at your first reunion meeting.
3. Set a date for a team reunion for members and their families. Usually about 3 to 4 weeks after you return is a good time.
4. At the team reunion, share the duplicate photos. Be sure to have everyone share their own "Woodyisms" and that "one special experience" that they recorded on the trip back home.
5. Prepare the team members for the joy and excitement in reliving your mission experience with others. Every team member should prepare for being asked to share their rich stories and experiences in your own church as well as surrounding churches, civic clubs or with whoever might request a presentation.
6. Continue the relationship building by maintaining correspondence with the hosting church.
7. Each team member should be a positive influence in their attitude about future mission trips and also encourage others to become involved in nearby mission

opportunities.

8. Be bold in your testimony and always be prepared to minister and serve wherever possible.

9. See that your trip is reported to the local media.

Some "Do's" and "Don'ts" for Mission
Do's:

1. Observe local customs about shaking hands (sometimes it is done on entering and on leaving), kissing on one or both cheeks (for women, giving *abrazos,* or hugs). If in doubt, ask your host to explain what is proper.

2. Eat what is offered, and do not ask or hint for anything not offered. (Luke 10:18)
   In most cultures, you should take time for polite conversation during your meal.

3. If any gift giving is done, do so discreetly and not ostentatiously. Ask your host what to do about giving to beggars, and follow that advice.

4. Be aware that in some cultures people maintain a different distance when engaged in conversation than we Americans do.

5. Be aware that in some countries, toilet paper should not be put in the toilet but must be put in the wastebasket. Ask if you are not sure. A stopped-up toilet is very unpleasant to deal with.

6. Learn as much of the local language as you can, and speak it whenever you can.

7. Be prepared for worship services that are very different from those you are accustomed to — either more formal or much less formal, even charismatic/Pentecostal. Sometimes very long.

8. Be prepared to give your personal testimony, to pray aloud, and possibly to preach.

9. Smile at all times and remember to keep your sense of humor about you!

Don'ts:

1. Don't take pictures of anything military unless your host says it's okay.
2. Don't waste water. Use it sparingly for showering, bathing, laundry, etc.
3. Don't waste food and don't make fun of the food that is set before you. Take what you want and always eat what you take. If you are being served, it is permissible to say "Just a little, please," or "No more, thank you."
4. Don't eat raw vegetables or unpeeled fruit unless they have been washed in water treated with chlorine or iodine.
5. Don't drink untreated water unless you know beyond the shadow of a doubt that the water is safe to drink (not just safe for the people who live there). Bottled water is available in most countries; boiling for 15-20 minutes is a good alternative; water purification tablets should be potent enough to guard against giardia as well as common bacteria.
6. Don't use ice, unless you know it is made with pure water.
7. Don't take any tobacco or any alcohol products of any kind.

Comprehensive List of Personal Items

This list has grown over the years. I believe that everything on this list is important and should be included. I have found that you will not wear half the clothes you take, so that should be considered. Pack as light as you can and remember that everything that you can leave behind with your hosting family or church is a testimony to your dedication for mission.

1. Medical forms and your international travel insurance cards.
2. Copies of your visas and your passport picture page for each piece of luggage, plus an extra copy in your passport pouch or wallet.
3. Passport pouch that goes around your neck or a money

belt and fanny pack.

4. Proper clothes (work, casual and dress, if needed). I suggest taking clothes that may be donated to a local church.

5. Suit coat. Even though you might not think that it is necessary, I have found that for church and worship services, the local people will probably expect you to at least wear a sport coat. You can also leave this when you are departing.

6. Shoes. I suggest that men take black tennis shoes. First of all, you will not look like a tourist and, second, they will pass as dress shoes for worship.

7. Hat for working in the sun, sunscreen, sunglasses.

8. Work gloves if needed.

9. Rain gear and a small fold-up umbrella.

10. Bath towels, washcloths, hand towels that can be left for your host family or church.

11. Sleeping bag and pillow. Also take a blow-up pillow for the airplane.

12. A small flashlight with extra batteries. Be prepared to also leave this. A flashlight is something that will be cherished as a valuable treasure!

13. Your camera with all the film you will need and extra batteries.

14. Your Bible, a small Bible commentary, your pens and pencils and journal book.

15. Collapsible drinking cup.

16. Cash in new or un-circulated currency. Plan on using cash even if the country accepts credit cards. It is safer and easier.

17. All your medications and copies of your prescriptions.

18. Insect repellent.

19. Toiletries: soap, shampoo, lotion, handy-wipes, small rolls of travel toilet paper, tissues. The travel toilet paper, tissues and handy-wipes should be carried with you at all times.

20. Travel alarm.
21. Your own personal snack foods.
22. Dictionary with both English and the language of the hosting country.
23. Two rolls of duct-tape, to give away.
24. Instant coffee, powdered creamer and sugar. Coffee is a precious item, so take one **plastic** jar to leave with your hosting family.
25. I always take my Swiss Army multi-purpose knife in its leather cover, inside my suitcase. (Don't try to carry it on). You will be amazed at how many times this handy device will be very helpful.
26. Host gift for each family that you will be staying with. All team members should spend about the same amount of money for gifts.
27. Photos of your entire family, including your pets. Take extras to give to your hosting families.
28. As many small hotel-type sewing kits as you can pack; to use, if necessary, but mostly to give away.
29. Extra hygiene items to leave: aspirin, toothpaste, tooth-brushes, soaps, shampoos, vitamins, brushes and combs.
30. A bottle of hydrogen peroxide to dip your toothbrush in for a cleaning.
31. Extra pair of your prescription eye glasses.
32. Your vaccination card from the local health department.
33. Desire to love as Christ loves!
34. Positive attitude and a teachable spirit.
35. Tolerant, flexible and patient spirit with a good sense of humor at all times.
36. Servant mentality.
37. Christ-like willingness to accept those who at times might be unpleasant and hard to accept.

Additional websites for
valuable mission information

All three of the following websites will be very helpful to the overall success of your mission experience. May I suggest that you check to see if one of the very important and informative UMVIM meetings is planned for your area? If so, it will be one of the best investments your team can make to prepare for your mission trip.

1. Website of Mission Volunteers at the General Board of Global Ministries, The United Methodist Church; general resources and information: http://gbgm-umc.org/vim/
2. List of UMVIM Coordinators for United Methodist Conferences in the USA; online documents and good references: http://gbgm-umc.org/vim/resource.htm
3. List of UMVIM Web pages for United Methodist Conferences in the USA, listed by state: http://gbgm-umc.org/connections/vimpages.html

IF YOU WOULD LIKE TO CONTACT THE AUTHOR
FOR ANY REASON, PLEASE FEEL FREE TO SEND
YOUR LETTER OR YOUR EMAIL TO:

WOODY WOODWARD
1430 East Sleepy Hollow Drive
Olathe, KS 66062
continentaltimberkcww@yahoo.com
caw328@sbcglobal.net